Praise for *Church of ...*

"This book is a luminous love song to the body of the earth, a sober celebration of interconnection, an elegant entreaty and a bold proposal for a new way, the renewal of the ancient way, a way of healing and holiness and prophetic enkindling. This book is a prayer. Intelligently shaped and beautifully written."

—Mirabai Starr, author of *God of Love* and *Wild Mercy*

"This book will be of great use to all who feel a little broken by the world right now—those of a Christian heritage especially, but really everyone yearning to reconnect with something larger. I think the wisest course of action would be to slip it into a knapsack and remove yourself outdoors to read it."

—Bill McKibben, author of many books including *Falter, Eaarth,* and *The End of Nature*

"Victoria Loorz has brought us her truth-telling, real 'kitchen table talk' in this book. It is deeply personal, inspirational, and spiritually nourishing. As you turn each page, you can feel yourself being called to get outside and connect with creation. Our natural altars—the trees, the waters, the sun, and the moon—are waiting to heal us."

—Veronica Kyle, cofounder of the EcoWomanist Institute

"*Church of the Wild* is about a very different church. There we encounter a wilderness that might be closer to us than our church buildings. Victoria Loorz's storytelling offers a Christ-tradition language much needed for new dialogues, and a path back to the parts of the Christian faith we have forgotten for centuries. Take and read, and let your body be-wild-ered."

—Cláudio Carvalhaes, theologian, liturgist, and author of *Liturgies from Below*

"Victoria Loorz has written a breathtaking book, bold and intimate, erudite and immensely loving. She does for Christian belief what Robin Wall Kimmerer did for scientific botany: invite it back into the ecstasy of a life lived together with all beings, into the poetry of sharing breath. Loorz has the gift of conveying profound messages in a light-hearted and light-footed—and outright beautiful—way that makes it impossible to put down the book. *Church of the Wild* is a groundbreaking account of post-dualistic religious experience, and an intoxicating temptation to allow yourself to love."

—Andreas Weber, biologist and author of *Matter and Desire: An Erotic Ecology*

"*Church of the Wild* is miraculous in its depth and beauty. Weaving rich storytelling with fascinating historical and theological insights, Victoria Loorz lays out a spiritual pathway rooted in communion with nature. Though Loorz is part of the Christ tradition, she speaks to all of us longing for an Earth-based spirituality. This is a sacred text for our troubled times."

—Mary Reynolds Thompson, founder of Live Your Wild Soul Story and author of *Reclaiming the Wild Soul*

"Victoria Loorz compassionately explores the people and ritual practices that remind us how sacred our planet is, for it is our first and foremost holy scripture. Her deep thinking and grand language offer us a great gift: the chance to renew our spiritual relationship with all of creation through exuberant and ethical engagement."

—Gary Paul Nabhan, aka Brother Coyote, Franciscan brother and author of *Jesus for Farmers and Fishers*

"A cascade of stories beautifully written, deeply personal, and refreshingly human. They invite us to create a narrative together for a transformed people fitted to a changed earth. Many of us have been waiting for this book. While it crisscrosses most everything, it is concretely about transformed churches, seminaries, and interfaith communities gathering to practice the future. Pass it on!"

—Larry Rasmussen, Reinhold Niebuhr Professor Emeritus of Social Ethics, Union Theological Seminary, New York City

Church of
the Wild

Church of the Wild

How Nature Invites Us into the Sacred

Victoria Loorz

Broadleaf Books
Minneapolis

CHURCH OF THE WILD
How Nature Invites Us into the Sacred

Published in association with The Bindery Agency, www.TheBindery Agency.com.

Lyrics to "God Outside and Inside" by John Slade used by permission.

Scripture quotations, unless otherwise indicated, are taken from the Holy Bible, New International Version`, NIV`. Copyright © 1973, 1978, 1984, 2011 by Biblica, Inc.` Used by permission of Zondervan. All rights reserved worldwide. www.zondervan.com The "NIV" and "New International Version" are trademarks registered in the United States Patent and Trademark Office by Biblica, Inc.`

Scripture quotations marked (WEB) are taken from the World English Bible™. Public domain.

Cover image: Olga Korneeva
Cover design: Laura Drew

Print ISBN: 978-1-5064-6964-5
eBook ISBN: 978-1-5064-6965-2

This book is dedicated to the wild ones who have heard the whispering call from Earth and Spirit to restore the great conversation.

Contents

Prologue

This is a story about a land where the trees talk and the waters croon and the people fall in love with birds, who love them back. This is a story about an enchanted forest hiding in plain sight, invisible until, somehow, the veil drops—and what was unseen can suddenly be seen. You may catch a glimpse when you cross the threshold on the far edge of the abandoned field, or when, just for a blinking instant, you notice how the brambles of the blackberry bush connect you to everything.

The ancestors knew this and reminded one another around their fires that they belonged to a great web of life. They were called into wilderness by a voice that spoke in words planted silently in their hearts, by the voices of the cedar trees, the lilies, the desert sands. Sacred voices tucked into pockets of the wind. Some of these ancestors were called out of Egypt, out of oppressive systems that didn't acknowledge their lives as valuable. Called into the wilderness to listen. To prepare. To be tested and encouraged and strengthened. There the wild creatures of the night, the fiery bushes and cool streams, and the manna that fell from the sky reminded the people of their true identity.

Once upon a time, all humans knew their lives, their food, their survival, their sense of meaning and kinship with God or the gods was connected with all their relations: the hawks and soil and ferns and mosquitoes. Like all the other wild creatures, they belonged to the land, and they knew it. They were untamed and self-willed and listened to their own intrinsic authority. They were part of a grand conversation, a relationship of reciprocity and respect, connecting them with all the other beings and elements of life.

But there came a time when some of the people could no longer hear the conversation. An elixir fell over the poppy fields, like Dorothy entering Oz, causing them to fall asleep. The wax in their ears became hardened, and their hearts pretended that they were happier controlling the world than loving it. They rushed right past the burning bushes on the way to Importance, missing the message of the doe hiding in plain sight with her newborn fawn. They packed the bodies of sacred forest cathedrals onto trucks and shipped them to mills. They forgot that the thrush songs spelled out warnings and wisdom in octaves. Disconnected little by little, their voices went missing in the symphony of aliveness. The songs of the wild God cascading through the trees no longer guided their lives. And a deep loneliness sunk down upon the people like a heavy fog nobody could see.

The time has come to lift that veil of fog and return to intimate relationship with the living world. More and more of us are taking our place, once again, as full participants in the web of life, which we remember is held together by love.

There are no magic words to incant, no spiritual laws to memorize, no ruby-slippered heels to click three times. You don't need to read a hundred new ecotheology books or leave the church or become an animist or pantheist. (But you can if you want to.) You simply need to learn how to listen. And allow your heart to be broken, just like you do every time you fall in love.

Because the holy is in your place too. You open the gates into this enchanted land, your home, with hands muddied from the soil outside your house and a raw, scabby, and unprotected heart. You enter naked and brave.

1
A Communion of Subjects

The divine communicates to us
primarily through the language of the natural world.
Not to hear the natural world is not to hear the divine.
                    —Thomas Berry, *The Sacred Universe*
                                    20th century CE

On the edge of the barranca, behind the 1970s Southern California suburb where I was a teenager, among the sagebrush and valley oaks, I had a Place. Before it was completely developed into million-dollar homes, this canyon's edge of the barranca was *my* Place. I never brought anyone else there. I never talked about it to anyone. It was a secret.

I liked the getting there nearly as much as the being there. The path wandered through tall-as-me wheat-looking weeds that squeaked when you pulled the heads out. Boulders and even taller brushes of scrubby sage and laurel sumac defined a particular path, a deer trail that looped around the edges of the barranca wall.

The entrance was appropriately hidden. To recognize it, you needed to train your eyes and leave markers like stones atop one another or a small ribbon tied to a broken branch. It took me several visits before the homing beacon of the Place would draw me there without annoying backtracking. But once I knew precisely where to pull aside the scratchy pointed leaves of the sprawling oak brush, my Place would be revealed. It was a small clearing on a scrubby cliff that looked out over a mysterious campground that I couldn't quite see.

The acoustics of the canyon allowed me to listen in on entire conversations of strangers at the campground who didn't realize the walls amplified their voices. I felt deliciously invisible, imagining whole lives of the unseen but clearly heard people beneath the rocks sixty feet below me.

But the humans were not my primary interest. The hawks were. The lizards and the spiders were. The cloud structures. The warm Santa Ana winds. A particular scrub jay stopped being a bird in the background and became a sacred other: one whom I encountered in second person. She became familiar to me, and I would look for her every time I visited.

I made a circle with rocks. And around that, a square with sticks. And inside the circle, a triangle with three branches. I was adapting a symbol I knew from YMCA camp: a cross in the middle of a triangle in the middle of a square in the middle of a circle. It just didn't look right to me, so I rearranged it. In the middle of the triangle, where the cross is supposed to go, was the space for me. From this vantage point, at the crest of the barranca cliff, protected by amulets of ritual I didn't fully understand, I would sit. And listen. And watch.

Twice a year, sheep grazed in the fields on the other side of the canyon. Sheep. In fields, baaing. Seriously. In my suburban California town. That doesn't happen anymore, but even then it felt surreal. They even had little cowbell collars. It was so enchanting that those sheep still show up in my dreams. In my world of swim meets, algebra exams, and long notes to my best friend left in her locker, these sheep were threshold totems, inviting me into another world.

Once, near dawn, a single, curious doe came to see what I was doing. She didn't notice me at first, but when our eyes locked, she didn't run. As we stared at each other, I saw her alarm melt into curiosity, and some kind of deep knowing passed between us. I didn't even try to understand it; I felt honored and grateful. It was a sacred moment, though I didn't use those words then.

I longed for her return every time I went to my Place. In fact, the hope of seeing her again was half the impetus to head out there at least once a week. She only returned once, which was a little disappointing and confusing, until I read about a similar encounter Mary Oliver captured in her poem, "The Place I Want to Get Back To." The poem, which is about a numinous visit by two does, explains that "such gifts, bestowed, can't be repeated." They can, however, become beacons to show you the way. Numinous presence through deer became an important beckoning toward the divine for me, a gentle nudge to pay attention.

I didn't know it then, but I was learning ceremony. I was learning to meditate. I was learning prayer. I was learning that God is found in the bushes, hidden from the trail, in communication with the birds and the wind, and in the trusting visit of the deer. My Place was slowly turning into *our* Place as I recognized that I belonged to a much larger story.

It took many years before I had a clue that this private ritual I had as a teenager was calling me into relationship with the land, the world, the sacred, and my own soul. I was unaware that the relationship I built with this particular place held the DNA for a calling and expression of vocation that would develop in my life. I didn't realize that this little sanctuary was an initiation into my own direct experience of God—my first church of the wild.

* * *

Nearly forty years later, a small group of brave souls launched Ojai Church of the Wild with me. I'd been imagining it for a few years: a way to redefine church and reconnect with nature by meeting outside, without walls that block out the rest of the world. Under a cathedral of live oak branches, the altar would be a mandala created with acorns and dried leaves and rusted bits of barbed wire. I longed for church to be a place where Mystery is experienced, not explained.

'The core of the service would be an invitation to wander on our own, to connect with the natural world at our own contemplative pace. We would find or create spiritual practices that re-member ourselves back into our home terrain as full participants. Reading from the "first book of God"—which is what the ancients called nature—the liturgies would include the whole world, not just humans. And instead of sermons from one preacher, we would learn how to enter into conversation with the living world. Sitting in a circle, not in rows, we would share our wanderings with one another and listen for the voice of the sacred in the sermons of the trees and the gnats and the crows.

And that's what we did. After twenty years as a pastor of traditional indoor churches, I walked out the chapel doors and into the sanctuary of the oak trees. A small group of us put ancient-yet-new spiritual practices into place that reconnect us with the living world as sacred. And called it church.

When I first founded Church of the Wild in Ojai, California, I felt a little insecure, like I was just making things up. But I wasn't. The idea of wild church was in the zeitgeist—a mysterious work of Spirit that had landed in the hearts of many across North America. And of course, this was nothing new to people whose spirituality had never been severed from the soil where they live.

Church of the wild is not a new, trendy form of church for people who shop at REI and backpack the Pacific Crest Trail. Gathering in this way is more than connecting with the natural world in order to reduce your blood pressure or obtain any of the other proven benefits of time spent in nature. It's not even a sneaky way to get religious people to care about climate change. It is a movement of people who are taking seriously the call from Spirit and from Earth to restore a dangerous fissure. Spirituality and nature are not separate.

This book is not about starting a wild church community—although you can if you want to and there are resources in the back of the book if you are interested. Rather, I hope this book encourages in you a *wild spirituality*.

I use the phrase *church of the wild* in a broader sense throughout these chapters. The word *wild* is not meant in the colloquial sense of "out of control." Rather, I use it to refer to the natural, innate way the world was created: not controlled or tamed or domesticated. Reclaiming *wild* is reclaiming who you are meant to be, who the world is meant to be, which isn't static. Wild means swirling in dynamic and even loving relationship because all wild things are naturally interconnected.

I use the word *church* as a place of intentional connection with the sacred. For some, *church* is a trigger word, recalling bad experiences. I understand that. But I think some words are worth recontextualizing. Placing *church* into a new context of *wild* instantly reframes it as a sacred space, outside of human-made buildings and dogmas and control.

I use the preposition *of* intentionally too. I mean that church is not just *in* the wild but *of* the wild. The sacred connection is fully in relationship with, and even initiated by, nature.

* * *

"We are in trouble because we do not have a good story," Catholic priest and evolutionary theologian Thomas Berry often said. "We are between stories. The old story is no longer effective. Yet we have not learned 'the new story.' We are talking only to ourselves. We are not talking to the rivers, we are not listening to the wind and stars. We have broken the great conversation. By breaking that conversation we have shattered the universe."

Over the last thirty years I've wrestled with this broken conversation as a pastor of indoor churches, a climate activist, a mother, and now as a guide who leads people in spiritual practices that reconnect them with the natural world. I've discovered something I've known deep down all along but never had the cultural, religious, or even internal permission to embrace: spirituality and nature are not separate. Attempts to keep them apart break the world.

This book is a prayer to help us restore that conversation. In doing so, we participate in the emergence of the new story. It will emerge through us.

The old story continues to be exposed as a story constructed in service to white supremacy and patriarchy. I'm writing this in the days of the COVID-19 pandemic, watching helplessly as forests on the West Coast burn and the ice in the Arctic melts. Ongoing police violence against Black people has triggered protests that are finally starting to wake up white people. At least some. There is not a single institution unaffected.

We are staring at the slow-motion collapse of an empire. Standing at the threshold of profound change.

We as a society are being asked to reckon with the reality that a select few have benefitted from a patriarchal society that has taken the gift of life on Earth and treated it as a right. Those in the dominant Western culture have demanded not just the fruit of the tree but the whole tree—and the water and sun and birds and beetles too—and consumed it all as if they were the only ones who mattered. As if the rest of Earth were here for their taking. For a person, group, or species to act as if they are the only ones who matter, they need to strip the inherent worth of those they wish to dominate and objectify them. Otherwise, domination is impossible.

Professor, philosopher, author, and visionary Carol Wayne White observed the same root of objectification underlying racial oppression, citing a "lethal combination of intimately conjoined white supremacy and species supremacy. . . . Both of these impulses—white supremacy and species supremacy—evoke a hierarchical model of nature built on the 'great chain of being' concept, and they have produced violent and harmful consequences."

The hierarchy that Dr. White names is deeply embedded in every aspect of our society and worldview. The needs and desires of those on the top of the pyramid are prioritized. Everyone and everything else is objectified and valued according to their usefulness by those on top. Forests become lumber. Cows become beef. Deer become game. Land becomes private property. People of color become cheap labor or a threat.

A false belief system of separation and dominance is opposed to every system of life, with disastrous consequences ecologically, spiritually, culturally, socially, economically, and every other -*ly* you can think of. These worldviews are so deeply embedded that it takes a lot of effort to even see them, much less change them.

The layers of crises and cruelty we face will not be solved with technological, political, or economic strategies alone. A deeper transformation of heart is necessary to welcome in a new story. Moving away from a worldview and a way of life that treats others as a "collection of objects" toward a new way of being human that participates honorably in a vast "communion of subjects" is what Thomas Berry calls "the Great Work."

The Great Work is spiritual at the core. Gus Speth, an environmental attorney, ecologist, and climate advocate, has summarized the problem brilliantly: "I used to think that top global environmental problems were biodiversity loss, ecosystem collapse, and climate change. . . . But I was wrong. The top environmental problems are selfishness, greed, and apathy, and to deal with these we need a spiritual and cultural transformation. And we scientists don't know how to do that."

Do we spiritual people know how to do that? I spent twenty plus years in church leadership, and spiritual transformation was rarely, if ever, connected with actual cultural change that addresses these problems. I also spent a dozen years as a nonprofit leader in the climate movement, where spiritual transformation meant something more like "engaging faith communities" in the campaign of the moment. But it rarely meant developing a new way of life, directed by a spirituality that deepened relationship with the land and waters and species we were seeking to protect.

* * *

Spiritual and cultural transformation is what I hoped church would be about when I went to seminary thirty years ago. My first job after graduation was with World Vision, a global Christian humanitarian organization, in their advocacy and education department. For the entire year I was pregnant with my son, I researched and wrote a comprehensive tool kit to encourage churches to "care for creation." That was the language we used back then, in our attempt to shift from a worldview of dominion over nature (the traditional view) to stewardship of nature (a still inadequate framing, as it retains the place of humans at the top of a hierarchy). The kit, called *Let the Earth Be Glad*, was sent to fifty thousand evangelical churches.

Books on the topic of creation care were being published, with authors like Matthew Fox and Thomas Berry offering compelling ecocentric theologies and asking worldview-shifting questions. Though this was before much discussion on the connection between fossil fuels and the climate crisis, ecological problems like deforestation and polluted air and water were clearly harming the children and families World Vision served.

The tool kit included all kinds of items and ideas for churches—from exegetical studies and scriptural references of nature's revelation of God (Job 12:7, for example: "but ask the animals, and they will teach you; / or speak to the land, and it will inform you") to projects for kids to learn about Jesus by considering the lilies and frogs. We even included a cassette tape (it was a long time ago!) with nature sounds that churches could play during worship services. I was determined to encourage church leaders to bring nature *inside* to open the hearts of their congregants so they would care about nature *outside* our doors. I had to emphasize the impact on humans, how the children of poverty-stricken countries were harmed by ecological degradation. Attempting to stay grounded in love rather than fear, the kit opened with this psalm:

> Let the heavens rejoice, let the Earth be glad;
> let the sea resound, and all that is in it.
> Let the fields be jubilant, and everything in them;
> let all the trees of the forest sing for joy.

While the design and language of the kit seemed clearly within the boundaries of orthodox Christianity, I knew it would meet resistance. A whole section of the kit was essentially a defense: "No, we aren't saying you should worship the creation rather than the Creator. No, this isn't a liberal agenda. No, . . ." On top of that, the development department at World Vision was particularly nervous. One of their top donors was the Weyerhaeuser family, who owned the largest timber production businesses in the world. I was warned by the head of fundraising that this kit better not upset them. The fact that their multibillion-dollar income came from "converting" more than thirteen million acres of forest into products for human consumption created a challenge for my project. It's tricky to talk about letting the trees sing for joy while they're stacked on the back of a semitruck.

Honoring the inherent spiritual value of the trees and the creatures of the forests was a politically charged line to walk three decades ago, just as it is today. I tried to navigate this line by opening the kit with a quote from an unlikely ecotheologian—a young girl from the beginning of the twentieth century who was neither liberal nor conservative. In 1902, Opal Whiteley was five years old and living in a logging town in Oregon. She kept a journal filled with old-soul intimacy with the natural world. And she knew this intimacy as Holy Presence.

> Morning is glad on the hills.
> The sky sings in blue tones.
> Little blue fluers are early blooming now.
> I do so like blue.
> It is glad everywhere. . . .
> The earth sings in green . . .
> I did stop by some grand fir trees to pray.
> When one does look looks up at the grand trees
> growing up almost to the sky,
> one does always have longings to pray.

In rural America at that time, children were often regarded as farmhands. Opal's talk of connecting with field mice and joining lichen in worship was severely misunderstood and even punished. Her journal was ripped into pieces by her sister a few years after she wrote these words, but Opal kept all the pieces. At age twenty, she meticulously reassembled the shreds like a puzzle when a publisher recognized the beauty of her words and offered to print a small run of a book.

I felt that Opal had a unique capacity for connection with the living world that was needed to break past the politics and resistance in the dominant evangelical church. Churchgoers needed words to engage their hearts. I included logic and statistics to satisfy the mind, but I sensed that the statistics and science would not bring about any kind of spiritual awakening. A heart-centered connection with the natural world was needed.

The *Let the Earth Be Glad* kit was beautiful. And well received. I'm not sure how much spiritual or religious transformation it accomplished, if any, yet it set me on a path that I continue to follow today. It's a path I suspect you may be following as well. We may be called "nature mystics," those who experience the presence of the sacred through nature.

Nearly a millennium ago, another nature mystic, Hildegard of Bingen, engaged the world with a similar intimacy. A Benedictine abbess and one of only four women who were named a doctor of the church, Hildegard's spirituality integrated mystical experiences with botanical knowledge, medicine, embodied desire, and music. Like Opal, Hildegard's connection with the presence of the sacred began when she was young and was experienced through nature. Sainted for her intensely intimate visions of God, she described the fecund, wild presence of Christ as *viriditas*, which can be translated as something like the greening power of the divine, pulsating through all things. Not unlike Opal's earth singing in green, Hildegard wrote,

> O most honored Greening Force,
> You who roots in the Sun;
> You who lights up, in shining serenity, within a wheel
> that earthly excellence fails to comprehend.
> You are enfolded
> in the weaving of divine mysteries.
> You redden like the dawn
> and you burn: flame of the Sun.

Separated by eight hundred years, these two women expressed a common mystical experience of the sacred nature of nature. Their words, like those of other mystics throughout history, invite us into a sacred conversation with the natural world.

* * *

My personal spirituality is rooted in the Christ tradition— a term I prefer over *Christian*, which is a label I find difficult to swallow these days. Rather, I see myself as an "edge walker," wandering along the hemlines of the Christ tradition. I stand at the inside edge of a tradition that has brought many people, including me, deep pain and has also brought many people, including me, deep joy and meaning. I've adopted this term, *edge walker*, from nature writer Terry Tempest Williams. The *Encyclopedia of Religion and Nature* describes her edge walking as traveling "the narrow space between the religious tradition she credits for having 'forged her soul,' and her direct and very personal experiences in nature that have revealed a truth of their own."

Perhaps you are an edge walker too. Edge walkers occupy a thin space and are by definition a bit lonely. Most people inhabit the vast spaces on both sides of edges. But those of us called to the thresholds—the edges between—live in this thin space and recognize one another when we meet. The edges between biosystems are called *ecotones*. These thresholds usually contain the most biodiversity and therefore are the most resilient. A shoreline, for example, is the ecotone edge between the water and the land. Matter from the sea and the terrestrial shore is exchanged in these intertidal zones, inviting more life-forms to flourish.

Those of us called to the ecotoned edges need one another. Kurt Vonnegut calls this kind of connection a *karass*, a word he made up that means "a network or group of people who are somehow affiliated or linked spiritually." The time is coming soon when the edges we inhabit will start to redefine the center. And we will need to lean on and learn from one another as we, together, engage in the work of that redefining. Each of us is characterized by our own unique gifts, communities of influence, and a particular bio-region. But we cannot behave as silos. The more diverse our relationships are, the more resiliently we can hold our own individual edges.

Every religion has an edge where the mystics live. I once attended a conference organized by Ed Bastian, a Buddhist mystic whose calling is defined by his deep respect for and encouragement of interfaith spirituality. He gathered spiritual leaders from diverse traditions to consider what we had most in common: living on the same planet. Cynthia Bourgeault was the spokesperson for the Christian tradition. She was joined by Jewish mystic Rami Shapiro; Sufi practitioners Kabir and Camille Helminski and their whirling dervish friends; Pravrajika Vrajaprana, a Hindu nun from the Vedanta convent; and Don "Four Arrows" Jacobs, a Native American college professor and activist for Indigenous rights.

We talked about how our faith traditions could connect us with the actual soil and water and creatures of Earth. And how that connection could be a spiritual foundation for the environmental movement. What I remember most was a golden thread of mystical connection with divine presence that all of us expressed in our relationships with the natural world. Even in our diversity, we all felt that we had more in common with one another—edge walkers from other traditions—than we did with people more firmly planted in the center of our own faiths. "Theologians may quarrel, but the mystics of the world speak the same language," Meister Eckhart observed in the fourteenth century.

There have always been edge walkers: those who didn't follow along with the status quo, who didn't swallow the version of religion offered by those on top of the hierarchy as The Only Way. And at that edge, spirituality and nature are in unbroken relationship. Mirabai Starr, herself a feminine mystic, can articulate this direct experience with the sacred in nature with a candor that is alluring and accessible: "A mystic is someone who has an experience of union with The One—and The One may be God, it may be Mother Earth, it may be the cosmos. That experience is rare, but everyone has them I think, where you momentarily forget that you are a separate ego, personality, self, and you experience your interconnectedness with all that is."

A recent study demonstrates what Starr intuits. The study, seeking to learn the spirituality patterns of Americans, showed that nearly six in ten adults often feel a "deep connection with nature and the earth," whether they are affiliated with a religious community or not. It is my experience that most people have stories of a mystical encounter in nature—a time in which the veil of disconnection dropped and they were able to experience their deep belonging to an interconnected and sacred Earth. But those of us caught in the dominant Western worldview do not have enough of a cultural context or a language to know what to do with those encounters.

* * *

After the *Let the Earth Be Glad* kits were sent out back in 1994, I was invited to be part of a small group of Christian environmentalists who were gathering at Au Sable Institute, a Christian ecological retreat center in Michigan. This was my first trip to the Midwest, and as a Southern Californian, my first encounter with an actual autumn. Giant maple leaves in colors I'd only seen before in crayons—brilliant cadmium oranges, alizarin crimson, and yellow ochre—covered every stitch of dirt and sidewalk. They created a vibrant, pulsating mosaic that looked more like an impossible thousand-piece puzzle than it did real life.

It was hard for me to fully pay attention to the meeting with the leaf opera going on outside. But the group of us, twenty or so, sat at a conference table to discuss the ways we could engage the church in advocacy measures around the worsening ecological crises.

We discussed an article written twenty-five years earlier by a historian from UCLA, Lynn White Jr., who indicted Christianity as the primary culprit in determining our ecological crises. White cited the "Christian axiom that nature has no reason for existence save to serve man," as the primary force that continues to define our political, economic, and even ecclesial beliefs and practices. It was an awakening for me to see that Christianity not only has resisted engagement on environmental issues for political and otherwise confusing reasons but has also been responsible for much of the worldview of hierarchy and separation itself.

If my unreliable memory serves, my only real contributions to the discussion were periodic flashes of defensiveness: "How dare he blame us Christians for this mess!" And something like "hrumph" or other exceedingly unhelpful and clueless things. To be fair, I was also a wee delirious from lack of sleep. My three-month-old son, Alec, whom I'd brought with me, caught his first cold on the plane and couldn't nurse well. I don't think I slept the entire conference.

Though my mind was foggy, it was an *apocalyptic* moment for me, a moment of unveiling what has always been there. I needed to see how the Christian religion not only has colluded with the agendas of empire after empire throughout history (as it still does today) but is often used as a weapon of mass destruction. In this case, a justification for mass destruction of the planet since, hey, heaven is our *real* home.

I remember we all soberly accepted Professor White's critique and felt a responsibility as Christian leaders to do something. The discussion focused on helpful ideas and plans, and we all made earnest and well-intended commitments to one another and to God and the dancing golden leaves (or maybe that was just me). We committed to doing everything in our power to awaken the church to the crisis happening outside our doors.

But more than awakening needs to happen. What we neglected to discuss at that meeting took me another twenty years to see. The very real, concrete changes our world desperately needs, but desperately resists, will not happen without a compassionate and intimate reconnection with nature. What we need can't be legislated or explained or resolved through a great social media campaign. What is needed is something that is deeply seeded at the core of every religion: love.

Mystical experiences in nature—those moments when you sense your interconnection with all things—are more than just interesting encounters. They are invitations into relationship. Beyond caring for creation or stewarding Earth's "resources," it is entering into an actual relationship with particular places and beings of the living world that can provide an embodied, rooted foundation for transformation. The global shift necessary to actually survive the crises we've created depends on a deep inner change.

Restoring relationship is, I believe, the true mission of religion. The word *religion*, at its roots, means *re*, "again," and *ligios*, "connection," like ligaments. Religion is meant to offer us support to *connect again* what has been separated. Apparently we need constant reminders to continually reconnect with the fullness of life, the whole, the holy. What we've created is more like *disligion*: disconnection from people and species unlike us. When religion loses its purpose and colludes with the forces of separation instead, it becomes irrelevant and even irreverent.

* * *

Through my love story, woven into the pages of this book, I invite you to honor your own experiences of falling in love with the world. Well, not with "the whole world" because that's too big. But with particular beings: those trees who live on your block, a certain crow who frequents your street, the shoreline on the edge of the village. Our neighbors.

The spiritual transformation that both scientists and spiritual people are all calling for is not about bringing nature inside for the church to remember that God's love covers everything. It's not about having churches play nature sounds on cassette tapes. It's about going outside and spending time with the other beloved ones of Earth and offering our tender, gracious attention to their needs as well as our own. That's what you do when you fall in love. This connection will give us the courage and the energy and even the ideas we need to challenge our prevailing consumerist mindset for the healing and restoration of our world. As simplistic as it sounds, I believe that only love is strong enough to bring about the change we need.

The new story is emerging, and I cannot pretend to know all the layers. Yet one aspect that seems essential relates to the worldview of belonging—a way of being human that acts as if we belong to a community larger than our own family, race, class, and culture, and larger even than our own species. The apocalyptic unveiling happening in our world right now makes it difficult even for those who have been sheltered in privilege to look away from the reality, both tragic and beautiful, that we are all deeply interconnected. Humans, trees, oceans, deer, viruses, bees. God.

Many people, whether they go to church regularly or avoid it, feel closest to God while they are in nature. Even a simple gaze at a full moon can be a spiritual experience if you are mindful enough. And a glorious sunset can summon hallelujahs from deep in your soul. Humans are made to engage in life-affirming conversation with the whole, holy web of life.

Those who self-identify as spiritual but not religious have told me that nature is already their church. They've said, "If this wild church had been an option for me, maybe I would not have left religion." I understand. And relate. Many have been wounded, disappointed, betrayed by the institutional church or by the people who misuse the power that the institution of church gives them.

Nature, powerful though she is, doesn't abuse her power. Re-placing our spirituality back into the actual sacred world, where it has been rooted for most of history, is a way to restore our place in a more primal power embedded in systems of Earth. Wild church re-places a human "kingdom" paradigm of hierarchy, monarchy, and inequality with the power systems of Earth, which can be described as a "kin-dom" of cooperation and kindred reciprocity.

Church of the wild is one way to help us live into a new story of a kin-dom of God that includes the whole system of life and regards all humans and all species as inherently good and valuable. In this kin-dom we love neighbors—all neighbors—as ourselves. We do unto others—all others—as we would have them do unto us.

Can the world be saved by love alone? It sounds nice, like a meme with a sunset in the background. Some may want to call this a spiritual bypass: in our current state of crisis, the need for immediate and active resolution is real. Against what odds, in these coming days of unraveling, can love prevail? How can a civilization based on domination and control and selfishness and all the other disturbing things wrong with our society change into literally its opposite—before we succeed in destroying the entire planet? It's implausible. And yet the preposterous transformative power of love at the core of nearly every religion, including my own, may just be the only way through.

2
When You Realize Something Is Missing

My Beloved, the mountains, / and lonely wooded valleys . . . //
. . . the supper that refreshes, and deepens love. . . .
. . . She feels that all things are God.
     —Saint John of the Cross, *Spiritual Canticle*
         16th century CE

Five years ago, when I first started imagining church that wasn't in a windowless building, it wasn't because I was a particularly outdoorsy, backpacker type. I went camping for the first time after I graduated from high school. And even though I get giddy whenever I see any wild animal or a bright-red fallen leaf, I manage to kill all indoor plants and can't identify a single mushroom. I would survive in the wilderness for like ten minutes if civilization ended suddenly.

I began this journey in response to a longing and—as cliché as it may sound—to a calling. My journey into a

wild spirituality began after nearly twenty years of leading churches and a dozen years coleading a youth climate
nonprofit with my son. In both roles—as a pastor and an
activist—trying to keep my spirituality and love of nature
separate led me into a dissatisfied unrest and ultimately
burnout. I discovered on a very personal scale that when
spirituality is severed from the rest of the living world, there
are severe consequences for the aliveness of both the people
and the rest of the world. Like all new life, though, an ending was necessary to create empty space for a beginning.

Church burnout is not uncommon, particularly for
idealistic pastors like me. In fact, I think "leaving church"
(as Barbara Brown Taylor describes in her book of the same
name) is a natural phase of spiritual growth. There comes a
point when you need to withdraw from what has become
too familiar in order to see again.

Activism burnout is not uncommon either, particularly
for idealistic youth. Working for change that can rarely
be seen in a lifetime, when we only have one lifetime, is
inherently difficult. There comes a point when you need
to withdraw in order to know who you are again. And
remember what you are fighting for.

* * *

My mother took my sister and me to church occasionally
when we were growing up. I thought about baby Jesus
every Christmas as I placed him in the little manger and
listened to the "Hallelujah Chorus" on Easter. But my

young soul's sense of connection with God, or Mystery, was defined by an unnamed feeling of belonging that was never part of any church service.

My family moved a lot, so I had to get used to making friends quickly and then letting them go easily. In each new town, my sister and I would seek out playmates by knocking on doors and asking if there were any children our age who could come out and play. But my actual sense of belonging in each new suburban neighborhood would come from a different search. I would seek outside the boundaries of my yard for a place I could call my own.

We never lived near the woods or on a farm with acres of wild open space. But the little pockets of dirt on the edge of new construction, an empty field through a broken fence, or even the mud dams in the "creek" that formed along the curb after the rain offered me solitude at the wild edges of my domesticated life. These were spaces where I felt seen, fully myself, and connected—although by what, and to what, I could not have articulated. I didn't have religious language for encounters like the ones I experienced as a teen in my Place at the edge of the barranca. But these are the places where I experienced a numinous and very wild presence I later identified as God.

The God I discovered as a Christian convert in my twenties was not tame. Jesus was fierce and raw and real and full of a love I could hardly contain, much less fold up into four spiritual laws. The best way to describe this conversion is to say that I fell in love. Hard. The kind of love to which you surrender everything: I actively threw away vestiges of my old life—often in the literal trash can. This intense new beloved had no room for old lovers clinging to the edges of my psyche. I broke up with my friends and my boyfriend for a new faith community, one full of people who were also pursuing their sense of meaning and identity through relationship with Jesus.

I gave up my identity and my career as a young professional too. I was moving up the corporate and creative ladder at Walt Disney Studios, but I left after a couple years of this new religious fervor to go to seminary. And after a year of seminary, I nearly left even that to become a nun at an ecumenical monastery in the Ozark Mountains. I've been accused of being intense. Idealistic. A romantic. I admit it. But I wanted to say *yes* to this ravishing new love in the most boundless way possible.

* * *

Before I learned that people in my new church only read the books found in certain kinds of Christian bookstores, I discovered a small Catholic–retreat center bookstore near me. I was magnetically drawn to books by cloistered people who lived a long time ago. Turns out they were all mystics. To Saint Therese of Lisieux, the "Little Flower"; Brother Lawrence, a cook in a monastery who could practice the presence of God while washing dishes; and the anonymous author of the mystical *Cloud of Unknowing*, written in the 1300s. The first Christian book I read was *Dark Night of the Soul* by Saint John of the Cross. It went straight over my head, but my heart felt at home.

That sweet night: a secret.
Nobody saw me;
I did not see a thing.
No other light, no other guide
Than the one burning in my heart.
This light led the way
More clearly than the risen sun
To where he was waiting for me
The one I knew so intimately—
In a place where no one could find us.

This hiding place, this secret intimacy, resonated with my experiences in nature. Now I had a name for that presence. A tradition. The church offered a very real feeling of belonging. I had a clan and a language and a culture.

But with the new religion, I also had a new set of boundaries. And rules. And a building. Places in nature weren't exactly considered a place to connect with God. Nature was nice and to be appreciated, but God was not in the trees. Those who worshiped trees were pagans and heretics, and you needed to be careful out in the forest, which is where the devil worshipers go to sacrifice cats.

Sure, our congregations would go to retreat centers in lovely mountain locations, and there would often be time for a walk—later, you know, after the Spiritual Time of Actual Worship that happens with good music and a great preacher who calls us all back into relationship with Jesus. In that world, the real spirituality happens in a building. Or a closet. Blocking out the rest of the world. Hallelujah.

One of the only books in the Christian bookstore at the megachurch I attended that I found to be interesting was an evangelical classic called *Celebration of Discipline*. Discipline was something that didn't come naturally to me, and it was apparently an important part of being Christian, so I bought the book and planned my very own first solo prayer adventure. I filled my backpack with water, a blanket, no food except for a granola bar that tasted like cardboard in case I got a headache, my sketchbook and zipper pouch of colored pencils, and a sweater. Oh, and my Bible; I didn't go anywhere without my Bible in those days. And I got into my car with a plan: I'd drive to a nearby town with trees and a cascading river, and I'd curl up next to a welcoming oak tree and commune with God. It would be grand.

I ended up in a little town called Ojai and decided to walk along the trail next to the park until I found the precise image I had in my mind, expecting downright holiness. The specificity of the image in my mind should have been my first red flag. Nothing was quite *it*. I was convinced that just around the bend, down this ravine, off the trail, back on the trail, over that next hill . . . *there* would be the clear and perfect place. Instead, I spent the day judging it: Too close to the trail. Too many other people. Not enough shade. Too much poison oak. Too loud.

Every place I rejected brought more and more distress. I could no longer even see the great California oaks, beaming with pride at their own sturdy magnificence. The squirrels and rabbits, snakes and scrub jays were not even in my peripheral vision. I was on a mission, dammit.

After a couple hours of this, exhausted and annoyed, I gave up, defeated. Back near my car, I tossed my bag and my bones down on the grass in front of an uninteresting, overlooked oak tree. There I ate my uninteresting granola bar even though I didn't have a headache. I didn't even care anymore that at least four other people were invading my solitude. The whole thing was now officially dumb.

Mad at myself for having twisted this perfectly lovely adventure into a fruitless search for something perfect that doesn't exist, I heard a voice, sort of, inside my head: "Draw me." I took out my pencils and began to sketch the contours of the oak tree in front of me, even though it was surrounded by concrete and invaded by a noisy playground. I began to see the squirrels and birds that lived in the tree, the layers of life she was supporting. I noticed her elegant branches that, in some places, bent all the way to the ground, as if offering herself to the whole little park, as mothers do.

As I continued to settle down, allowing myself to notice and pay attention, a voice welled up in me again—a voice that I interpreted then as God but that I think now may also have been the tree herself. The voice said, "You could spend your entire life looking from tree to tree and indeed, someday, you may find a more perfect one to sketch. But you will have spent your life looking and never seeing. Stop and love what is right before you."

When I returned home, I shared my experience with a couple of my new church friends, who quickly warned me that God is found in the Scriptures, not in the trees. They labeled it *pantheism*, which they said was bad. God is not a tree. End of story. I looked it up and found the definition confusing because pantheism didn't seem bad to me: "God in all things." But I was not in touch with my own inner authority then. And there was so much fear around paganism and animism and pantheism in my church circles that I didn't want to admit to my church friends that my spirituality was grounded in the ground, not in the sky somewhere beyond the planet.

While it was never specifically taught as doctrine, the understanding that spirit and nature were dualistically separate was baked into the spirituality of the churches I attended. To regard a tree with animate and sacred presence was threatening, somehow, to an invisible and jealous god that demanded full and unquestioning devotion and obedience. Without a cultural context to value it, I buried the message from the tree somewhere inside me. Eventually I stopped talking about my connection with nature altogether. It became just another thing that I left behind to follow Jesus.

* * *

Seminary was a chance to immerse myself in the Christian story. I loved my Greek and New Testament and church history classes. By my second year, after deciding not to move to the monastery, I left the conservative church that had transitioned me into the tradition and leaned toward more progressive churches. I was the editor for the campus newspaper and took out massive student loans so I could fully soak in seminary life. I reveled in long theological discussions with other students and even met my husband there and got married before graduation.

A couple things were never presented or discussed in the seminary curriculum: first of all, the religion's insidious relationship with patriarchy, racism, and empire was never mentioned. The menace of patriarchy haunted me, unseen in the shadows, for another twenty years of working in the church before I began to even identify it. The other subject I was hoping to learn more about, but didn't, was the process of transformation that had upended and redirected my life. I wanted not to simply learn *about* it but learn how to invite other people into their own journeys of transformation to become more fully who they were created to be. The closest I could come was a concentration they called "spiritual formation."

A focus on spiritual formation meant that I took jobs in mostly independent, nondenominational churches where I could do cool contemplative kinds of things—centering prayer, retreats, small groups, midrash discussions, Bible studies, Taizé chants. Every Good Friday for several years I built an elaborate labyrinth in the sanctuary, complete with interactive stations where you could write poems, light candles, and bury lamentations in a wailing wall constructed with at least sixty heavy stones I'd drag up in a wheelbarrow from the river bottom. And candles. Lots of candles. Hildegard chants played overhead. It was cool. I loved it. People came. They said it was cool.

But I wasn't longing for cool. I wanted tears and psalm-ish anger and genuine wrestling with the disconnect we felt in our lives and the world. I wanted *authentic*. I didn't want *formation*, which began to feel like trying to tame people into a mold. I wanted *trans*formation: where people's lives and character and values were changed, freed from the domesticating forces of culture and our own internalized limitations. The root prefix *trans* means "through" or "across," meaning we are formed as we move through the ways life changes us: from life through death to new life. Transformed, metamorphosed to be more like who we truly are meant to be. Which is another way to say *more wild*.

I served as the first female pastor of a progressiveish church in a wealthy ski town in the Colorado Rockies, when my kids were little and my marriage was rocky. A year or so into the job, I decided it was time for me to break out of the confines of the routine and expected ways we did church—just a little—with a series on Genesis and creation and new beginnings. On the first Sunday of the series, people filed into a dark room with the chairs chaotically arranged facing every direction.

I had spent all day Saturday covering the floor-to-ceiling windows (a rare church with big windows looking onto the forest) with black butcher paper and disarranging the chairs, preparing the space to experience the first day of creation: the inclusion of light and order with the preexisting chaos and darkness. Not the replacement of chaos and darkness, mind you; the *inclusion* of it in the act of creation. Both belong.

"And the land was chaos, formless and empty, and darkness was over the face of the deep, and the spirit of God was moving gently, nurturing, brooding over the face of the waters." I love this image: there is no rejection of the chaos, the darkness. There is love and maternal care and an acknowledgment that both the dark and the upcoming light are holy. During the service, I turned the lights on gradually and removed the paper in layers from the windows. Congregants were invited to arrange the chairs into a new order. It was a little annoying when they chose to reorder their chairs back into the same facing-forward-in-rows manner; but overall, I was pretty dang happy with my creativity. People who attended had begun to imagine the cosmology story in a new, more relevant way.

The board members, though? Not so much. My satisfaction with myself was short lived. One of the major donors of the church complained that I was a "tree-hugging dirt worshiper." I guess it was supposed to be an insult (one I've since fully embraced and worn on my car as a bumper sticker). They were concerned that my unconventional ideas and connection with nature were pulling me away from the orthodoxy of the church.

But nature didn't pull me away from the church; church pushed me away from the church.

I remember a particular moment in another church, where I was again the first female associate pastor, leading a weekly small group. No matter what the topic, people kept getting stuck on an old, entrenched image of God that no number of progressive sermons or interactive labyrinth experiences could shift. One man I will call Joe came every week to remind us all that the Richard Rohr book we were reading together was all gibberish to him. I finally asked him directly one week, "So what is your image of God?"

His reply made the room go into slow motion for me: "God created the world. Then left. The rest is up to us."

Sometimes awakenings feel glorious, like an *aha!* that starts from your toes, shivers through your body, and exalts itself through the top of your head. Sometimes, though, awakenings feel more like a slow-motion sucker punch: a heavy, tingling feeling that sinks into your body from your head down and rests like a puddle of mud underneath your feet. Grounding you.

Joe's reveal of his image of God—secured by years of consistent attendance at a progressive church and faithful participation in all of my oh-so-spiritual gatherings—was, for me, one of those sinking awakening moments. His declaration of the absence of God in the world, and the rest of the group's general agreement, made the room feel distorted.

My eyes were drawn to the peeling multicolored plastic, pretending to be stained glass, covering the only window. Many churches are built like this, with few or no windows, in line with the Roman architectural objective of shutting out the rest of the world. Homes for the wealthy were built with courtyards, where the plants and flowers could be controlled and domesticated. All windows faced the courtyard. No windows faced outward. Church architecture adopted this design for centuries. The idea is that "what is holy is in *here*, not out *there*."

God created the world and then disappeared. The words lingered in the air, and all we had left was that fake, peeling stained glass, blocking the only window to the rest of the world. I broke the awkward silence in the room and told everyone to go outside. Stare at the stars for the last half hour of our gathering, I told them. It was one of those irrational decisions. I didn't explain why, but I could think of no other response.

Some said later that it was the first time they had looked at the stars in years.

* * *

I left my pastoral position at the church, and my marriage, which was already crumbling, ended. I moved back to California with my kids and started working a corporate job again. I was convinced that my clergy days were over. At least I'd have a real paycheck. I thought I could just find us a nice little church where we could visit every once in a while to stay connected. Which is to say I dragged my kids to every church in town. For months.

After church (and sometimes during the service), I'd have grumpy things to say. I didn't like the sermons. I didn't like how nobody greeted us. I hated the forced "peace be with you" at the beginning. I especially complained when the building was just too suffocating. Or there were no humans within forty years of my children's ages. I complained about the whole setup: one person, the pastor, telling his (it was usually his) opinions about stories from more than two thousand years ago, peppered with "relevant" stories from daily life. I'd whine about the patriarchal, imperial lyrics of the songs. "All Hail King Jesus," for random example. And I could no longer repeat a creed with words like "true God from true God, begotten, not made, being of one substance with the Father" that made no intellectual or emotional sense to me.

Church used to feel rich and alive, but little by little, what happened inside the building felt flat. I couldn't even read the stories I loved anymore. Once so important to me that practically every page was highlighted, underlined, question marked, exclamation pointed, and hearted, the Bible had become stolid and stagnant. Everything about church annoyed me, but I couldn't really articulate why or what to do about it.

Finally, one day my ten-year-old son observed, "Just admit it, Mom; you hate church."

All I could muster was a lame denial, "Nuh uh." Which is what you say when your kid nails you between the eyes. I didn't hate church. Not really. But I no longer felt I belonged.

Sometimes the best way through an impassable brick wall blocking your path is to walk away for a while. To stop trying. To allow the unknowing to compost in the darkness within you. I knew something was missing. Something was being asked of me that I couldn't name. I suspected it wasn't *just* me being critical. Don't you hate that feeling? It feels like true *dis*-ease: an inability to feel ease. It's a frustrating inability to understand what is happening that eventually leads to gradual surrender, if you're smart. I ended up leaving ministry—and the church completely—for seven years.

* * *

One of the primary reasons I initially became a pastor was that I liked how friends and family and work were all mushed together. I resented the silos dividing work and home, and I'd raised my kids without that divider until my divorce.

As a single parent, I found I needed to build up the silos in my calendar between my work and my kids. I also had to erect walls in my heart so I didn't spend the whole day in tears about all I was missing from my kids' lives. One day, a couple years into the new single-motherhood life, I realized I didn't cry when I missed a school play. The silos were affecting my connection with my children. I knew I had to find my way back out of the corporate world. So when I and most of the staff were laid off, I felt equal measures of relief and fear.

We moved to a smaller house, and as I went through my too-many books in preparation for a mega garage sale, I wistfully gave away my Thomas Berry, Bill McKibben, and Matthew Fox books, thinking those days of ecology and spirit were over for me. I didn't, however, pack away the DVD of Al Gore's *An Inconvenient Truth*. I figured casually that my then twelve-year-old son, Alec, who liked volcanoes and earth science, would enjoy watching it. Sometimes your mind is clueless about what Mystery has in mind.

We watched the film the next night. When the DVD was finished, my daughter and I left the living room, but Alec stayed. And watched the whole film again. Then all the special features. And he went to bed, silent.

The next day he was on fire, insisting that his classmates help him "stop global warming." His best friend, from a family that regularly watched Fox News, pushed back, calling Al Gore a liar and the climate crisis a hoax. Infuriated, Alec came home that afternoon and immersed himself in internet research to create his own climate presentation.

His presentation, finished around midnight, was called "The Five Flavors of Climate Denial." He researched all the excuses his friend offered and then some. He dug up photos, science, and answers to each of the denial memes. The next day at recess, he delivered his presentation to prove his friend wrong.

Encouraging his passion, I searched for an organization for him to get involved in the climate movement. At the time, virtually nothing existed for youth. I did find a group of teachers in San Diego who were holding a climate conference for their high school students. I called to ask if Alec could attend, even though he was still in middle school. When they heard about his enthusiasm and Power-Point presentation, they invited him to lead a workshop.

On the day of the conference, the keynote speaker was caught in traffic and couldn't make it, so they asked Alec to step in. He asked me what "keynote speaker" meant before stumbling his way through that first public presentation. It was the last one I ever solicited. In his passion, he had found his voice. After that, an avalanche of invitations came in, from rallies to sustainability conferences to TEDx Talks, from schools to Congress to corporations to the United Nations.

Within a few months, I set aside my side jobs to focus on the overwhelming need for the youth voice in the climate movement. We started a nonprofit called Kids vs.

Global Warming, which was later renamed iMatter. Alec's speeches addressed the science and harsh reality of the climate crisis in an accessible way. He was able to focus his audiences on the sober reality that the worst of the crisis will befall his generation, but he left them feeling like their engagement was not only necessary but meaningful.

Alec discovered his gift. Just today I received a book about youth in the climate movement that describes him well: "Alec's voice was already a commanding one, and he had the poise and conviction of someone who spoke from the heart. His ability to understand what was happening to the environment and to translate it into a message that inspired people was especially unique, both for the person and the era."

The youth voice was in demand. Alec quit school by eighth grade so that we could spend half of nearly every month on the road. He was learning more, we reasoned, by doing this work than he would in school. Together we organized youth-led marches in two hundred cities, filed climate lawsuits in fifty states, and supported hundreds of young leaders as they worked to pass climate inheritance resolutions at their city councils. Alec won numerous international awards, short films were made, and hundreds of news articles followed his progress.

* * *

On the fortieth anniversary of Earth Day in Washington, DC, Alec spoke from the giant stage along with dozens of celebrities, scientists, activists, and performers. Several hundred thousand people gathered at the national mall that year. There were hundreds of booths, tents with interactive maps showing sea-level rise, and giveaways of LED light bulbs and canvas bags. There were petitions and marches and flash mobs and table after table of nonprofits working hard to attract signatures and donors.

Alec's message from the stage ended, as it always did, with a call to "live as if our future matters!" Roaring applause. Our iMatter tent highlighted the youth plaintiffs for the federal climate lawsuit we were organizing. We hung huge mounted posters, showed videos of our projects, and offered a place where the kids could write to senators and be added to our database. There was a protest-sign-making table and a bandana that you could print "iMatter" on and wear for the iMatter March. It was cool. We got a bunch of signatures. People came. They said it was cool.

But we weren't longing for cool. We wanted tears and anger and genuine wrestling with the disconnect between humans and the world. We wanted authentic transformation. The whole thing cost tens of thousands of dollars and thousands of hours. By the end, we looked at one another blankly and realized we hadn't eaten anything all day.

Afterward, we had several blocks to walk to get to our car in the impossible traffic of downtown DC. On our way, above the din of impatient drivers and frenetic crowd cacophony, we heard a panicked call from what turned out to be a mama duck. Somehow she had found a nice, safe place to lay her eggs at least a dozen blocks from the danger of snapping turtles in the pond in front of the Lincoln Memorial. The problem was that getting her brood back to the pond without flying meant walking them straight in front of several hundred cars. Following her quacks, we found her anxiously encouraging her chicks to jump up a small curb (in other words: yelling with fear and panic like when you lose your four-year-old in Target by looking away for a tenth of a second). But her dozen tiny fluffs were too small to jump the four-inch barrier and were stuck.

My nephew found a box in a trash bin, and we collected all the peeping babies—which, by the way, if you haven't held a baby duckling, I need to mention how magical it is to hold these tiny creatures who weigh less than a tissue. It was tricky. Normally, you should leave Mama Duck alone in her arduous journey from the nest to the pond because intervening can sometimes scare her away and thus orphan her clutch of infants. Unlike most wild animals, ducks are among those who have managed to survive the urban takeover of their habitat. But with gridlocked and aggressive traffic for at least ten blocks, this duck was in over her head. We decided to help her navigate the dangers of our human mechanical presence and help her get to the Lincoln pond by luring her with the box of her crying fluffy chicks.

The kids stopped the traffic, and I carried the box of babies just ahead of the mama duck—far enough away that she would follow, but not too far that she might get confused and fly away. Once we got to the edge of the water, she jumped in from the three-foot wall, and we, as gently as we could, plopped all twelve babies into the water next to her. Good deed done.

Here's the thing: I think we accomplished more in the simple act of listening to what was needed—helping a family in distress because of the very problems being talked about in the Earth Day speeches—than we did with all the chanting and the swag. We were practicing Alec's mantra to live as if our future, and the future of all beings, matters.

* * *

It all seems almost like another life now, nearly a decade later. As I write this, I am sitting in a coffee shop on a random Friday in Bellingham, Washington, and I see three police motorcycles stopping traffic as several hundred high school students march down the street with signs like "No one is too small to make a difference," a quote from the sixteen-year-old international climate leader Greta Thunberg. I'm listening to the same chants we chanted a decade ago and feeling a mix of nostalgia and relief that this is no longer my life. I'm grateful to have contributed in some way to the work of empowering youth, who are now leading the climate movement. I also worry about the costs.

Greta, at age eight, was first awakening to the crisis at the same time, almost to the month, that Alec, at seventeen, was burning out. After years of authentic but naive optimism and a resolute hope that he and others from his generation really *could* make a difference, he began to recognize the depth of the climate tragedy and witness the sting of political resistance and the public shrug of indifference. I'm not sure which was more discouraging.

Even as Alec was growing in stature (finally maxing out at six feet, seven inches at age eighteen), winning awards, and traveling internationally to speak to larger and larger audiences, my son's spirit was diminishing. The years of the constant and exhausting hustle were taking their toll. Discouraged and disillusioned, we were both suffering from overwhelming exhaustion.

Alec ended up moving to British Columbia for college, a university set on the edge of a stunning old-growth forest. He didn't talk about his climate work. He didn't want people to know who he was. He cancelled most of his speeches and enjoyed being "one of the students" rather than the one on stage. The forest, the waterfall, the squirrels and ferns and mushrooms offered restoration and healing from the years of activism and travel and fame in the climate subculture.

By his second year, he was feeling energy again to organize an event in the forest. It was to be a twenty-four-hour spring equinox event, complete with an all-night campfire. With spring only a week away, Alec went to the woods after class. He was stopped by guards at the trailhead. There, he watched as his beloved forest was clear-cut. He listened as the birds cried sounds that he'd never heard before or since, a lament of terror. He watched as more creatures than he'd ever seen in one place sought refuge in the small pocket of woods that was left near the university. And when no other students showed up for the grief ceremony he and a couple friends planned, he could no longer hold it together. Quitting school, he came home to collapse. For four months, he rarely made it out of bed.

Burnout is almost built into activism. The sheer amount of energy and time and money needed to pull off each campaign is incredible. We choose a particular instrumental change from the millions that need to happen, create a strategy, design the campaign, identify the enemy, come up with an easy-enough ask, raise the money, show up for interviews, write blogs, shoot more videos, shout more loudly, and measure success by the number of new names in our database and followers on social media. Because, really, can we measure our success by an aggregate CO_2 decline? No. That's too discouraging. Even with all that the movement has accomplished, the CO_2 imbalance keeps increasing. So we stay focused on the goals before us, measuring success by metrics that don't matter. And once one campaign is finished, it's time to start over with the next one.

It's like trying to move a mountain one pebble at a time. Everyone is so busy and overworked and underfunded that we hardly have time to touch the very earth we are working so hard to get people to protect.

Herein lies the problem.

* * *

Like an ancestor who gathered berries and nuts, who knew which mushrooms were poisonous and which would be delicious, I had collected glimpses of "something missing" inside my heart for many years. The fibers of the basket were unlacing, and it was getting too heavy to carry. It was time to unpack it. Sometimes it takes years of collecting moments of insight before you are ready to dump it all out onto the table to see what you've got, find the patterns, make connections, and allow yourself to see what you never noticed before. The burnout I felt after years of church leadership and environmental activism—both of them disconnected from an intimate relationality with nature—offered me the opportunity to pay attention.

David Whyte tells the story of his own burnout. He felt called to leave the successful and meaningful environmental nonprofit he had created to devote himself full time to poetry, a difficult transition to explain to your partner. Exhausted by the back-and-forth wrestling with what to do, he met his friend, Brother David Steindl-Rast, a Benedictine monk, at a cabin in the woods, where they regularly hung out together. Brother David was able to clarify the problem. He said, "You know that the antidote to exhaustion is not necessarily rest? . . . The antidote to exhaustion is *wholeheartedness*."

I was halfhearted. I couldn't escape a gnawing discomfort lodging itself in my solar plexus as I wrestled with the division. I felt I could neither stay in nor leave the Christian tradition. A growing love for the natural world, and unprocessed, accumulated grief from the activism and the ecological crises themselves made both doing and not doing environmental activism impossible. The only solution seemed to be to leave nature for church or to leave church for nature. But I could do neither.

This phenomenon, I learned, was not unique to me. According to a recent study, people who are religious, spiritual, and "green" often feel that one part of their life or the other needs to stay hidden. At a climate-rally planning meeting, they don't admit that they go to church. At church, they don't admit that they planned the climate rally.

A *USA Today* article entitled "God Competes Against Mother Nature on Sundays" echoes this dualistic decision people feel forced to make. Citing a Baylor University study, the article explains how researchers overlaid amenities like nice weather, access to trails, and water areas with the percentage of people involved with religious institutions. They found an overwhelming connection between *access* to nature and *avoidance* of church. The growing number of "nones" (those without church affiliation) find nature a better church than a building and an institution. Nature, according to the researchers, provides for this group a "personal, subjective, non-institutionalized, and unmediated experience with the sacred. . . . When a person hikes in a forest to connect with the sacred, she or he may not feel the need to affiliate with a religious organization because her or his spiritual demands are met."

I don't agree that church or nature exist to meet our spiritual *demands*. It's just so . . . entitled. But that's beside the point. The blatant assumption in our culture that we must choose between church and nature helped me see the uncomfortable polarity more clearly. There must be a way, I thought, to challenge this false competition—some practice to help us re-place our spirituality into deep relationship with the rest of the world.

I remember one moment, after burnout from the church and the activism left me empty. I was lying under a giant live oak tree I visited often whom I called Mama Oak, looking up into her layers of branches to the clouds. Even as the prickly dried oak leaves made sure I wasn't too comfortable, I felt an unexpected wave of gratitude. The realization that I could no longer live with a divided heart was an invitation to stop and just listen.

In the emptiness, I began to feel new life stirring. New questions blossoming. Lying there on the oak leaves on a hot summer day, tempered by the shadow of the oak's massive branches, I heard an echo of the gentle voice of the mystic canticle of Saint John of the Cross: "My beloved . . . all things are God."

3
Into the Mountains to Pray

All has been consecrated.
The creatures in the forest know this,

the earth does, the seas do, the clouds know
as does the heart full of
love.

Strange a priest would rob us of this
knowledge

and then empower himself
with the ability

to make holy what
already was.

—Catherine of Siena, "Consecrated"
14th century CE

Once I was able to see with the eyes of the mystic and rely on my own inner authority to know the undeniable presence of the sacred in the natural world, I began to see a third way. The polarities of nature or church gave way to a new vision that sought to include the riches of my religious tradition but transcend the distortions. Church of the Wild became that third way. It was an experiment to challenge the centuries of priests who empowered themselves, like Catherine of Siena observed, with the ability to decide what was holy and what was not, and to develop new spiritual practices to heal the long-suffered divide. I needed to dig beneath the layers of patriarchy and power that have distorted the wild message of the Christ of my tradition to see if the duality of spirit and nature was inherently baked into my religious tradition or not.

In my years of preaching for indoor churches, I would spiritualize wilderness as a metaphor for tough times and "dark nights of the soul"—those depressions, disappointments, divorces, or deaths that we all have to face eventually. Wilderness, though, is more than a metaphor. I began to wonder what role the *actual* wilderness played in biblical stories. From Moses to Jesus, and from Hagar to Isaiah to Paul, the uncompromising directive from God to enter the wilderness at a pivotal moment in history had to mean something more than internal wrestling with ego or demons.

What role did the actual physical dirt and heat and burning bushes and wild creatures play in these transformational moments in history and in the developmental journeys of the people?

As we face our own epic historical moment, with cultural and biological systems collapsing around us, what role does the actual wild world play in our collective and personal transformation? Is it possible that a wild spirituality, antithetical to patriarchal traditions of the church, might actually be native to the message and heart of Jesus?

* * *

Jesus went into the mountains to pray. This fact seems important. Matthew, Mark, and Luke, the first three books in the New Testament, all mention it. So, it makes sense that learning how to pray is a big agenda for churches. Centering prayer. Taizé prayer. Silent prayer. Petition prayer. Liturgical prayer. Confession prayer. Prayer-without-ceasing prayer. Prayers of the people prayer. But when was the last time you were taught how to go to the mountain? Jesus didn't go to the buildings to pray. Jesus went to a mountain—or along the lakeshore, or to the wilderness. For some reason (well, for many reasons), *that* part of the spiritual journey is generally ignored.

I practiced prayer without mountains quite well for many years, thank you very much. In every pastoral position I've held, I've made sure that I got to lead different kinds of contemplative prayer experiences. I had a walk-in closet for years that I transformed into a groovy prayer room, where I could shut the door and have my prayer time, complete with candles on the altar and photos of people I particularly wanted God to pay attention to. The closet was my hidden, quiet place. It helped me focus. I figured it met the "went into the mountains to pray" criteria well enough. The stories couldn't mean that the *actual* mountains and deserts and wilderness had any significance, right? In all my church experience and throughout my seminary years, nobody—including me—ever talked about the role of the physical, material mountains and lilies in spiritual life.

I was pretty good at mountains without prayer too. Even at church. As pastor of the church in the Rocky Mountains, I and my congregation did all kinds of mountain outings together. Pretty much everyone in Breckenridge lives there because of the powder ski days, the aspen forests, the hikes to waterfalls, and the fourteeners (a term that all the mega-athletes populating this town knew but that took me six months to figure out: mountains to climb that are over fourteen thousand feet above sea level, yes of course). The natural world was, at best, an "environment" we appreciated. But our spirituality in no way integrated these mountains.

As I look again at the stories from my tradition with new lenses—ones that don't make a metaphor out of every mention of the natural world—I can't *not* see a green thread woven through the whole story of God. I've realized that it's not just that the wilderness invites us into the presence of the sacred; there's the mysterious reality that the sacred also calls us into the wilderness.

The word *wilderness* is used more than three hundred times in the Bible. I used to preach that the word *wilderness*

(Greek: *erémos*), referenced as a hot, barren, and desolate desert in Palestine, was a metaphor for the spiritual situation in which dark nights happen in your soul. But when we set the metaphors aside, we see that *wilderness* is actually a word to describe a real, physical place that is not populated by humans. The wilderness in the Mediterranean where these stories originated is not the Sahara desert that Hollywood versions of the stories want you to imagine. Rather, it was alive with growing plants, trees, and rivers, a place where shepherds could bring their sheep.

God sends people into the wilderness. On purpose. The call into the wild was issued to nearly every single leader in the Bible! God revealed God's self to Moses not in the tabernacle but in a bush, in the wind, on the top of a mountain. The enslaved people escaping from Egypt were sent into the wilderness—not the promised land—for forty years. Hagar escaped the jealousy of Sarah in the wilderness. Elijah fled alone to the wilderness to escape Jezebel's pursuit. Jonah tried to run from his calling and was consumed by a wild mammal of the sea, then heard a clear message from a gourd plant that was shielding him in the wilderness.

I kept looking. Job, Abraham, Isaiah, Joshua, Solomon, Hosea, Ezekiel—all of them were sent into the wilderness. Even the New Testament continues this thread: John, Jesus, Paul—at a pivotal moment in their lives, they were called into service by first being thrust into the wild. How had I not seen this before?

* * *

I kept digging and found that in each of the four narratives about Jesus in the New Testament, there is a clear connection between nature and spirit. Luke's Gospel locates the opening story of Jesus outside of the urban culture of humans: in a manger, a feeding trough for animals. While we re-create nativity scenes with thatched houses to resemble the barns and wooden troughs we imagine as the cradle for baby Jesus, many scholars from as early as the second century understood that mangers were found in caves. Outside the city. Found all over Palestine, these caves were used by herdsmen as stalls for their flocks.

So imagine, instead, Mary going through labor on the cave floor. Her son is born outside the edges of Joseph's ancestral land, away from their home, in the presence of cows, donkeys, and sheep. It is here where a deeper sense of belonging, beyond their religion and family, is presented. The baby is welcomed by animals and outcast sheepherders who dwell in the wilderness, expanding the character of home and belonging.

Matthew's Gospel emphasizes the wilderness by the third chapter when the wild man John is described. He is depicted as wearing a camel-hair tunic with a leather belt. I want to know why camel hair. Every sermon I've heard about this detail positions John as something like a crazy man, eating bugs and wearing uncomfortable clothes. But camel hair is actually very soft, almost like cashmere. Purveyors of wool say that of all the cashmere-like fabrics, camel hair provides the best insulation, which must be why the "barbarians" of the north, the Berbers, in the first century made their tents and cloaks out of it.

John wore camel hair for the same reason he ate foods of the wilderness: locusts and wild honey. He didn't just *visit* the wilderness to baptize people; he *lived* there. The point is made purposefully and repeatedly. John the Baptist was clearly a practitioner of wild spirituality, listening to the voice of the sacred directly, from within the embrace of the wilderness. And he was calling people into the wilderness as well.

John is said to have been fulfilling the message of the prophet Isaiah, "A voice of one calling: / 'In the wilderness prepare / the way for the Lord.'" In the wilderness, the Isaiah passage says, we prepare the way. But when the same translators repeated Isaiah's message in Matthew, they decided to change the punctuation. The quote was changed to "A voice of one calling in the wilderness, / 'Prepare the way for the Lord.'" This small detail places the reference to wilderness on the location of the voice rather than the location of the preparations that must be made.

John's message is one that should draw all the followers of Jesus into the literal wilderness, too, for their own preparation. But translators and preachers have deemphasized this part of the message, collaborating with a long history of detachment from nature. It's one thing to accept that John's spirituality was deeply grounded in the wilderness. But the idea that people might be called into the wilderness themselves to prepare the way? That is riskier.

* * *

Mark's Gospel begins with this same story of the wild man John coming to "prepare the way in the wilderness," alluding to the location of the upcoming initiation through the river and then the wilderness for Jesus to prepare for his public ministry. Avoiding civilization altogether, John drew people outside the boundaries of the village, baptizing them in the wild River Jordan. Mark locates the baptism scene "*in* the wilderness." The word used for *in* (Greek: ἐν) is a locator word and refers to a position in and among. John was *in* the wilderness, an actual place. This must be important. Mark wanted to make sure you'd remember it. The first chapter of his Gospel uses the word *wilderness* nine times.

My former next-door neighbor Ched Myers, a theologian, activist, and author of a brilliant political commentary on Mark, mentioned something one Sunday when we were gathered at his house for farm church—a version of wild church rooted in a local farm. He mentioned a small prepositional nuance in Mark's baptism story that introduced a profound shift in my perspective. I love big secrets hidden in small words. Listen to this.

Mark used the preposition *in* (ἐν: "in, a location") to locate the particular place where John was baptizing people: in the River Jordan. The people were baptized *in* (ἐν) the river. Ched pointed out that Jesus, on the other hand, was baptized *into* (εἰς: "into, a penetration of or union with") the river. And then a wild bird descended *into* (εἰς) Jesus, who was then sent *into* (εἰς) the wilderness. The Greek preposition εἰς is not positional. It is *relational*.

This distinction in the Greek is akin to the difference between being *from* a place and being *of* a place. It's the difference between "I'm from California" and "I love, care for, depend on, and am an integral part of a particular place that is in California." It's the difference between hiking *to* a waterfall by hiking along a trail in the forest and consciously walking *into* a forest by investing time and attention to really get to know the waterfall, season after season, and establishing an authentic relationship.

This is precisely why church *of* the wild is not called church *in* the wild. We aren't just meeting outside *in* a lovely location. When we gather as wild churches—among the cedar trees, oak groves, city parks, or desert shade—we are entering into relationship with our place. We are expanding our experience of prayer, and we are also learning how and why Jesus went into the mountain to do it. There is an unmediated presence of God that can only be experienced outside the human constructs of civilization when we enter into reverent relationship with the natural world.

So Jesus was baptized in the same location as the others: the River Jordan. But the writers of the sacred story used this word, εἰς, to emphasize that the baptism of Jesus was different. It initiated him *into* relationship with the wild river. *Into*, εἰς, *penetration*, *union with*: these are mystical and even erotic words of deep connection, words that take seriously the call to love and belong to a place. Baptism into a river is a wilderness immersion that initiates an intimate, vulnerable union with the living world.

Ecotheologian Lisa Dahill is passionate about this point and challenges the church to reclaim the early church's practice of baptism into local waters. Addressing members of the American Academy of Religion in 2015, she asserted, "The early church, like John the Baptist, practiced baptism in the rivers available: that was what 'living water' meant—flowing water, a connection to a larger fullness of life . . . baptized into the full wildness of the world and its flourishing, and into this particular degraded or intact watershed. It is utterly *immersive*." Jesus was baptized into the full wildness of the world, and we are invited there too. This vision expands the commitment of the sacrament. No longer is this simply a baptismal commitment to your own private spiritual journey or even to the spiritual connection with those within your religious community. This is an immersion *into* the waterfall, into real relationship with all the creatures of and in the actual waters of one's baptism, and into a commitment toward the thriving of the whole creative and alive planet.

* * *

Ched Myers wrote that Jesus was grounded into "the storied Jordan watershed of his ancestors through which Creator still speaks." We aren't used to this kind of animate relationship with the living world, where the Creator still speaks in the dialect of desert and dandelion and deer. But our spiritual ancestors were intimately familiar with it. This idea of conversation with nature is even embedded in the Hebrew language.

A friend of mine and her Israeli husband attended a Church of the Wild gathering with me one Sunday a few years ago. Afterward they told me that the Hebrew word *midbar*, usually translated as "wilderness," is rooted in the verb *dabar*, which means "speaking." *Ba-midbar*, my friends finished explaining to me, translated in most cases as *the wilderness*, also means "the organ which speaks."

Wait. What?

I raced home to check my beloved Hebrew-English lexicon, bound in fake maroon leather (one of the only books I still have from seminary), and I'll be damned if it wasn't true. The online lexicon agreed. Look, here's the direct listing in the *Brown-Driver-Briggs Hebrew and English Lexicon*: "midbar מִדְבָּר. *Noun Masculine. Definition: mouth. 1. mouth, the organ of speech. 2. wilderness.*" I sat back in my chair and let it sink in.

"Therefore I led them out of Egypt and brought them into the wilderness (*midbar*)." Holy cow. Rather than simply a harsh backdrop for a human drama, like we often portray the site of forty years of Israel's wandering, the wilderness as a place that speaks completely changes the tone of the story. What if God knows that there is simply no better way to rehabilitate from the effects of trauma than immersing into the wilderness? Seeing the wilderness as an organ of speech—the part of the body of living Earth that *speaks*—transforms it from a harsh place of difficulty into a tender place of intimacy.

I've felt that intimacy before. There is something about being in a wildish place for an extended time. First the silence allows you to hear your own voice beneath the chatter of distractions and to-do lists and self-evaluations. Then even that fades, and you can hear the voices of the wind and the rain and the chickadees. Eventually you can hear it: a deeper silence. The invitation to listen to the voice of the sacred. A voice that is deeply your own and also the trees and also God.

What if Moses and his traumatized people were sent into wilderness not as some sort of mocking punishment or intense object lesson? What if the wilderness was instead the place to listen to the sacred speaking through the voices of burning bushes, calling humans to remember that they belonged to a greater story? Exodus reports that the Israelites were captive under Egyptian colonization for more than four hundred years. Unlearning an identity of oppression and restoring a new character of belonging and purpose probably takes at least forty years. Rather than a punishment, being sent into wilderness becomes a provision, an opportunity for listening and deepening relationship.

So, too, for Jesus's forty days in the wilderness. God had just lavished praise and affirmation onto Jesus—in the form of a wild bird, mind you! And immediately, according to Matthew, the Spirit lead Jesus into the wilderness "so that the accusing one could test him."

Jesus was called *into* deep relationship with—union with—the wild. The divine voice spoke to him there, through the bodies of wild animals, desert sands, angels, and sun and stars. He needed this support as he faced his accuser, *diabolos* in Greek. You know the one—that inner critic, accuser, adversary—intent on keeping us distracted and safe from the dangers of prophetic leadership. Brené Brown simply calls that one "shame." Depth psychologist Bill Plotkin calls that voice the "loyal soldier": a subpersonality we all have whose role in your psyche is to keep you safe. And small.

In order to handle this intense internal wrestling, Jesus needed the support of the wilderness. Not the temple. Not the community. Just the wilderness, alone. The wilderness is the place to go when you are standing at the threshold, like Jesus was, of a calling that asks you to risk everything and embody all you are created to be.

In the wilderness—the place that speaks—you find that you are not alone.

Mark's story says, "He was with the wild animals and the angels, who were serving him." This is my translation from the Greek text. I made no changes to the words. I only removed a semicolon that most translations place between the wild animals and the angels. And it changes the whole meaning. Since the ancient Greek did not have punctuation, it's up to the translators to decide where to place the commas and the periods. The witty title of Lynne Truss's little book—*Eats, Shoots and Leaves: The Zero Tolerance Approach to Punctuation*—demonstrates the power that punctuation carries to shape meaning.

Placing a semicolon between the wild animals and the angels pits them against each other. The earthbound wild animals become part of the drama—the danger in a danger-filled hero's journey. The unembodied angels become part of the resolution—they care for Jesus. Adding a semicolon changes the meaning to something like this: "Jesus was with the *wild* animals (*Eek!* Another challenge!); but no worries: the angels ministered to him."

Why is it easier for us to believe that an invisible angel watches over us than it is to believe that a wild bird could show compassion?

Can we reimagine this scene for a second? The Sacred compels Jesus into an actual place called the wilderness of Judea. The beloved Son is sent there for a vision quest: an important test of character that all men (women, too, in some cultures) faced before taking on their full calling of leadership at important times of cultural transformation. In order to help Jesus reckon with the temptations to abuse power that are common to men (women, too, but not as much), the wilderness provided the unmediated support of the sacred through the land and the wild animals and the angels. Wild animals do not exist solely for that purpose, of course; animals and all elements of the wilderness (I guess that must include angels too) have their own inherent value and purpose in the interconnected story of aliveness. Yet in a very real way, the wilderness cares for you as you do the deep descent work of facing your own shadow as well as your true identity.

* * *

As I reimagine the wilderness in this more tender way, I can understand why Jesus repeated this act of penetrating relationship with the wilderness throughout his life. *Jesus went into the mountains to pray.* I looked up every single reference of Jesus going to pray that occurs in the four Gospels. Only once is the preposition *in* used to make a point about the location of the prayer spot. Every other reference uses the more intimate preposition of union and relationship, as in the baptism stories: Jesus went *into* the mountain, the lake, a garden beyond a particular winter stream, the wilderness, and a solitary place to pray. His prayer place was the wilderness, yes. But he went there to enter *into* a union with the sacred, speaking through the wild elements there. Are we not also called to enter *into* relationship with the wild and the divine?

It's almost as if you can't understand prayer *or* mountains without practicing both together. It's not just about changing the location of prayer, as you know it, to the outdoors, any more than church of the wild is about doing church the way it has always been done, just outside. There is a mysterious union that happens when we enter into relationship with the wild and practice sacred conversation.

Recent science, along with movements such as Japanese forest bathing (*shinrin-yoku*), demonstrates that the act of immersing yourself in a forest, in the desert, or in the grass in your neighborhood park leads to lower blood pressure, calmer nerves, and a more focused mind. It is good that people are waking up to the benefits of connecting with nature for their own health and well-being. But it is more than that. The living world is where we can be opened up in receptivity to a divine encounter. There is an invitation here, offered to all of us: in order to listen for the holy, to engage in intimate conversation with the sacred, one goes into the wilderness.

I suspect you, too, have received your own call into the wild. When you wander in the wilderness, as our spiritual ancestors did, you detach from what you thought your life was all about, from those many identities you used to think were really you. Some of those identities, especially the ones pressed deep into your wounds, are hard to let go of. It will take more than a quick walk in the woods. It takes an investment of time and attention. But eventually you'll be asked to give up precisely all the things that aren't yours to keep anyway. And you'll be left with who you really are. And then you will be ready to enter the promised land.

There is a story in the Old Testament about Jacob, the younger brother who stole his older brother's blessing. He was hiding in the wilderness, waiting out his brother's wrath. He settled down to sleep one night, using a stone as a pillow—which, if you're living in the wild, is probably not an unusual act. He dreamed of angels going up and down a ladder to heaven and back down to Earth, connecting the two. And Yahweh (the Hebrew name for God that evokes the sound of your breath, breathing in and out) was there, telling him how all Earth is a gift and how all the kin—all the relatives, all the families of the ground, the soil, Earth—would be blessed through him. God said to Jacob, "I will not leave you." Jacob woke up and exclaimed with wonder, "Yahweh is in this place, and I didn't know it!"

I feel myself waking up and shouting, "It's all right there, right in my own tradition. And I didn't know it!"

Jacob's dream is Thomas Berry's dream and the dream of the generations alive today: Yahweh, the sacred, is in this place, my place, this whole planet, and I didn't know it. It was a repentance as much as a revelation for Jacob. And so much more for those of us alive today. Seeing the holiness of this place where we live is a call to all of us upon awakening.

The natural world—that world where we already belong—is an alluring invitation into the sacred, into relationship with something larger. And that very sacred presence invites us into the wild. The whole process is holy. It is a dynamic, a reciprocity, a loving conversation, a relationship—one that includes me and you and God and the whole wild, alive world.

4
Allured into the Wilderness

The soul is like a wild animal—tough, resilient, savvy, self-
sufficient and yet exceedingly shy.
If we want to see a wild animal, the last thing we should do is
to go crashing through the woods, shouting for the creature
to come out.
But if we are willing to walk quietly into the woods and
sit silently
for an hour or two at the base of a tree,
the creature we are waiting for may well emerge,
and out of the corner of an eye we will catch a glimpse
of the precious wildness we seek.
>   —Parker J. Palmer, *Let Your Life Speak*
>   21st century CE

The call into the wild is often alluring. You may sense
it for years, a murmuring in the wind you almost hear
calling your name. Maybe you start to spend more time

outdoors and find yourself walking more slowly and noticing more details when you go for a hike. You may interrupt
a conversation to draw attention to the Cooper's hawk who
lands on the wire over your head and take the time to go
outside to see the moon rise when it's full. Little captivat-
ing whispers. The prophets like Hosea knew this call into
wilderness: "Therefore I am now going to allure her," the
sacred voice said; "I will lead her into the wilderness / and
speak tenderly to her."

It usually begins with a bit of unlearning to overcome
a lifetime of compliance, of staying on the path, of rule
following. Often that happens through some kind of suffering: a failure, an illness, a divorce, a death, a burnout.
The domesticated, compliant life is unmasked as a fraud.
To be allured into wildness, you need to break past inner
judgments. You need to allow yourself to let go and surrender control. Allurement asks you to be receptive, to
hold your plans loosely, to allow mystery to interfere. It is a
necessary posture to hear the others, and the sacred, calling
to you. Allurement is balanced with a sense of danger. It's
not a physical kind of danger, not physical danger at all,
but danger to your identity, your old stories.

For me, the call into wilderness was initiated by a slow
exhaustion. The oak tree down my street, Mama Oak,
kept alluring me back under her branches to just sit there.
And listen. I even asked my therapist, an ecotherapist,
if we could meet there. He agreed, and we met under
her nurturing branches twice a month for over a year.
During that time, I felt a rising sense that I would find

healing and direction as I availed myself more and more of the wilderness.

As far as I know, only one psychologist has dedicated his life's work to understanding human development in the context of relationship with the rest of the natural world: Bill Plotkin. In *Nature and the Human Soul*, he created a model of human development and a path of transformation built on the inherent soul connections we humans have with nature—inherent because our souls, as well as our bodies, are *part* of nature. He says that all of us are "born to occupy a particular place in nature—a place in the Earth community . . . a unique ecological role, a singular way you can serve and nurture the web of life . . . as unique as that of any birch, bear, or beaver pond." Paging through my heavily marked-up copy now, I see in the margins of the introduction my notes written then: "#1: Get in sync with nature."

It was, indeed, a synchronicity that drew me to a nature-based soul immersion that Bill and his team at Animas Valley Institute offered, focused on facing and befriending your own shadow. The intensive is called "Sweet Darkness," from a David Whyte poem of the same name that had become guiding words for me. In a time of darkness, go *toward* the dark, Whyte says, for "there you can be sure you are not beyond love."

Over five days in southwest Colorado, Bill and his colleague, Sage, invited us into relationship with the unknown parts of ourselves through a series of practices, including daily wanderings on the land where we encountered the more-than-human others, as he called them. I could feel a transformative shift happening within me, and I knew that I had found what had been missing. This was what I'd been longing for: an authentic reconnection with myself and with God. It happened through intentional immersion with nature.

When I got home, I wrote to Bill to ask if he could share a list of other spiritual leaders who had been through his programs. Through those connections, the seeds of Seminary of the Wild began to take root. I met Brian Stafford, Matt Syrdal, and Bryan Smith, and together we began to imagine a seminary connected to the wild. It would be a "wild seedbed," which is the root meaning of the word *seminary*: a place of spiritual and cultural evolution, as we say on our website. We felt that spiritual leadership development—which is what the word *seminary* means now—needed to be rooted in the wilderness, just as it was for our spiritual ancestors. Eventually, after talking and experimenting and dreaming for five years, we created programs that would support people as they deepened their relationships with Earth, their true, re-wilded selves, and with a wild Christ in order to embody their "wild call" to serve the world.

* * *

Our first Seminary of the Wild experiment took place in the foothills of Colorado. Seven pastors and spiritual leaders gathered in a small retreat center about an hour east of Boulder, Colorado.

"Cross a threshold," Brian said. "And wander on the land until you feel drawn to a place that feels both alluring and dangerous. Once you get there, ask this other—this place or element or being—to have a conversation with you about your inner beloved." Uh. Okay?

I had read Bill Plotkin's book *Wild Mind* on the plane coming to Denver, so my brain, at least, understood the language of the invitation. Bill's explanation of the inner beloved used accessible words that resonated with me: the inner beloved is an archetype, the part of you who is your *guide to soul*. I think it is not much different from Thomas Merton's mystical language of *true self*, or what Carl Jung named the *anima* or *animus*. It is the *wild twin* that Martin Shaw talks about in his lyrical retelling of the ancient European myth, *"The Lindworm"*: "The part of ourselves that we generally shun or ignore to conform to societal norms."

Plotkin describes the inner beloved as that part of our psyche that is "irresistible because she possesses precisely what our everyday Ego doesn't but most needs for the experience of true aliveness." A conversation with the hidden, irresistible part of you can be drawn out in conversation with an other of the alive world who, exposing their own vulnerability, whispers your name.

The language of *love affair* and *beloved* is the vernacular of the mystic from most religions. The beloved is the main character in Song of Solomon, a book found right in the middle of the Bible. I cherish this book as a metaphor for relationship with the holy. And it is more than that. It is also a story of a physical love affair between a lover and

his beloved and a story of the romance between the lover
and the beloved within.

> My dove in the clefts of the rock,
>> in the hiding places on the mountainside,
> show me your face,
>> let me hear your voice;
> for your voice is sweet. . . .
>> I am my beloved's and my beloved is mine.

I'm beginning to get it: these relationships are all connected.

* * *

Having dumped our gear at the retreat center, we are sitting in a meadow that is so beautiful, I feel a little dizzy. I
suppose that comes both from the altitude shock as well
as from a giddy sense of adventure, as if my body knows
something my mind can't yet grasp. Just minutes ago, it
was hot and muggy enough to sit barefoot on top of my
jacket. But dark clouds are starting to roll in, and the air
grows heavy and savory with moisture. Rather than rushing
back inside, Brian casually offers the invitation to wander
about, on and off the trails, and find a place that feels both
alluring and dangerous. We are to have a couple-hours-long
conversation with our inner beloved.

I want to say, "Wait. You mean now? Did y'all notice the
thunder?" But I don't. I try to act nonchalant, like I go hiking
all the time when it's storming. I nod at Brian's invitation,
as if I understand what an "alluring and dangerous" place

looks like, and I pull on my jacket that's not waterproof because why would it be? I'm from Southern California where it practically never rains. Zipping up my cheap un-waterproofed boots, I set out onto the drizzly, damp trails on my own, the air animated with a sparkle of moist but warm breeze. I'm pretending not to notice that the other pastors, all men from Colorado, have legit waterproof North Face jackets with hoods and real hiking boots.

The unlearning has to happen before the learning. It begins the moment you step on the path. A path is no longer a roadway to hike or run somewhere else. In fact, hiking isn't the way at all. You wander slowly and intentionally. It is your full presence along the path that matters. It is an act of reverence, a saunter. John Muir hated the word *hike*. He urged people to *saunter*. "Away back in the Middle Ages," he told his friend once, "people used to go on pilgrimages to the Holy Land, and when people in the villages through which they passed asked where they were going, they would reply, 'A la sainte terre,' 'To the Holy Land.' And so they became known as sainte-terre-ers or saunterers. Now, these mountains are our Holy Land, and we ought to saunter through them reverently, not 'hike' through them." Wandering is a contemplative exercise of sauntering, drawing us into nature as a sacred practice.

We are invited to wander, or saunter, until a place or being, both alluring and dangerous feeling, "calls to us." It is a contemplative practice. Sauntering happens without rushing, allowing you to deeply listen and pay attention.

The well-worn path—the way others have gone—leads you to a place where you are uniquely invited to step off the trail. This is an invitation to depart from what is familiar and easy in order to step into what is wild and unknown. Eventually you come to the threshold, yours, and you pause there with particular reverence. Perhaps a rotting log blocks your way, or the creek invites you to take off your shoes (another act of reverence) and cross to the other side. Careful not to disturb fragile soil or baby plants still learning how to be hardy, you stand in silence, inviting your imagination and intuition to guide you, your sensuous body to lead you.

To do this sauntering, you need to let go of questions like, "What are we supposed to do again? Am I doing this right? What if nothing happens?" As you saunter, it's not like you decide, "Okay, that rickety bridge I saw on my way in: that seems alluring and dangerous, so I'll go there." When you approach the world like you're on a mission and you have your own agenda—to reach the top of the mountain, to get the job, to get your kids to school on time—you've lost the reverent cadence of a wandering. There's nothing wrong with rushing to get to work on time; it's just not reverence.

Reverence is slow and intentional. It allows awe to fill your lungs and bring tears to your eyes, and it floods your bloodstream with extra oxygen and energy. Wandering with reverence means you're looking at the world with softened eyes that no longer see others as objects of beauty or utility. Reverence allows you to behold the trees and waters and tiny ants as separate beings. The act of wandering—through a forest or a desert or an empty lot on the corner of your block—asks that your eyes shift to see the others who share this place as living beings. You acknowledge them as individuals who are as concerned about their own survival and enjoyment of life as you are about yours. They are as important to their relations as you are to yours. John O'Donohue, a Celtic poet, philosopher, and priest, wrote the book (in both senses of that phrase) on *Anam Cara*, or "soul friends," which is what this sauntering and wandering is all about. He says, "Reverence bestows dignity and it is only in the light of dignity that the beauty and mystery of a person will become visible." The same applies to seeing the dignity of a tree or a place or even yourself.

As I set out on my wander, I have in mind the water I've been hearing rush around the bend from where we have been sitting. I strategize: "I'll walk down the trail until I reach the creek, and then I'll settle down and journal there for a while and head back before the rain really starts dumping. I'll dry my boots and take a rest before everyone else gets back. It'll be great."

But dangerous allurement overrides all your plans. Wandering to allow yourself to be allured to a particular place or being is an embodied, walking prayer of contemplation and gratitude and praise. Allurement implies an attraction from an other—who is outside you—and a reverent and unlocked response from inside you.

In order to do this contemplative exercise of wandering, a countercultural leap of imagination is required. Even if you can't initially conjure this deferential respect for beings who are not human, just intending the posture of reverence makes room for relationship. This, in turn, makes room for the presence of the holy. According to O'Donohue, "What you encounter, recognize or discover depends to a large degree on the quality of your approach. . . . When we approach with reverence great things decide to approach us."

Great things approaching us—I love that so much. That's the allurement. Allurement asks me to open up my imaginative, embodied senses to believe that an other who lives on this land is actually interested in me and wants to not only meet me but strike up an intimate conversation with me. Could "nature," out there, really care about me?

Before I can overthink all this to death, a mule deer doe dashes across the trail, about twenty feet away. I instinctively chase after her. All my interesting ponderings about *alluring and dangerous* are gone, and all my plans to get down to the creek are instantly deleted. I just allow my body to lead. Reaching the place where the doe stepped off the trail and onto a smaller deer path, I indelicately scramble after her as she glides effortlessly up a small ridge. Turns out the nine-foot muddy ridge is my slippery threshold. This doe has just called me into a sacred conversation.

* * *

By the time I reach the top of the ridge, the drizzle has turned into respectable raindrops. I step into a little cluster of pine trees, and I feel the visceral sense of crossing over into what O'Donohue and other Irish writers call a "thin place." It's that liminal space where heaven and Earth touch. *Limin* actually means "threshold." It's the space where you cross over, where something is left behind and yet you are not fully in what is becoming. It is the space between worlds, between our everyday life and the deeper life of spirit and soul. I feel a sense of enchantment in this physical place. Yet the trees are just trees, and the clouds are just releasing water like they do, and the deer is just a deer. But you can feel it when reality shifts into something deeper. The liminal exists in an actual place.

Looking up after the scramble, I expect the doe to have disappeared, as creatures often do when you want to get near them. Instead, standing not fifteen feet in front of me, she is staring at me, as if she has been waiting for me to catch up. Stunned to be this close to a wild deer, I gaze back at her dark eyes and nose. Her forehead has a small black smudge like she's been blessed with ashes on Ash Wednesday, and she sports a white rump and tail. Otherwise, her body is smooth with tannish-brown fur, and I'm standing close enough I can see that her steady eyes are dark brown, almost black. I feel as if she is looking straight into me.

Tears welling up in my eyes, I lower my head in a bow. I want her to know I am not a predator, but I think she already understands this. We stare at each other in that deep, mysterious gaze that nature writer Aldo Leopold talks about experiencing when he encountered the "fierce green fire" in the dying eyes of a wild wolf. Only, the fierce green fire in this doe's eyes is more like a fierce brown inquisition, one that slowly softens into something like trust. After a few moments, she twitches her ears and turns her attention to the other sounds coming from my friends who are wandering farther up the trail.

I walk closer to a large pine tree that is offering her branches as an umbrella of generosity, and my three steps closer do not appear to bother the deer. Unconcerned by the rain or me, this wild creature makes a decision that unfolds me. Looking straight into my eyes, she buckles her front legs and then her back. And she lies down.

My heart stops, and there is a swirling feeling around my head that I've felt before in deep meditation, in the presence of the holy. All attempts to hold back the tears are overridden. Tears, I've experienced, are evidence of sacred presence and authentic love or any profound kindness. I stay still there by my tree, letting this moment sink into my heart as the wetness sinks through my jacket.

This is reverence, yes: a sense that although I am a visitor here, I also belong. I have been seen and accepted. I feel an unexpected calm, a knowing that I am not just standing *in* the forest; I am a small, insignificant, and yet important participant *of* the forest. I wonder if Jesus felt this way every time he went into the mountain to pray. A little mouse and a couple of her tiny children scamper past my feet, perhaps abandoning one hole that will get flooded for another one closer to the gentle tree who is sheltering me. Normally, a mouse might cause me to shriek a bit irrationally. But this is enchanted time, this is liminal space, and nothing feels exactly real anymore. I smile as the mouse family scurries by my feet.

Minutes pass. Twenty of them? A hundred and twenty? I can't tell anymore, but dusk passes into the first stages of darkness. I realize this doe is settling down for the night, and I remember that I'm expected back at the retreat center. Plus, I'm soaked and starting to get cold. It is time for me to go. I bow to her with gratitude, and she blinks at me without moving. As I take careful steps back onto the path, I hear a voice deep within me that I would normally attribute to the whisper of God. But a flicker of possibility expands within me, a nudge to consider that the voice may also have come from the doe herself, echoing my own inner beloved: "I am with you always."

* * *

When I return to share my experience with the other pastors, I hardly have the words. On one hand, it's not much of a story. "A deer lay down in the grass!" Wow. But these friends understand what we were doing out there. We know we were walking tenderly in unfamiliar territory. The guides and the other pastors affirm the experience for me, mirroring back my own sense of wonder for the honor of this wild encounter.

The next day we head back out for another wandering. For two hours, I see no deer, feel no special connection with anything, and start to doubt that my experience the night before held any mystical reality at all. Kicking at the dirt like a pouting child, I start back to the retreat center, where I will have nothing to share with the others.

Suddenly a thought stops me in the middle of the trail: I should have spoken to my inner beloved! And at that very moment, as it starts to drizzle again, a doe, not ten feet in front of me, jumps over the trail and up a small embankment. My heart leaps up to my head, and I have that same swirling feeling when something mystical happens and you feel like everything you know about reality is suddenly suspended. Did this deer just come here now, as I was thinking about her? There's no way.

This sense of expanded reality is disorienting. Extraordinary, and yet completely natural at the same time. At the top of the embankment, there she is. This friend, different from the doe I met the night before, has a dark, splotchy, curious, and open face. She is just standing there, as if my presence is naturally part of her day. And just like the previous night, we look into each other. Perhaps she is making sure I am not a predator. That's possible. But it doesn't feel that way. I detect no fear in her eyes. There is a calm that is serving to calm me as well—as if she is the guide, the elder who knows what is happening, and I the novice.

After a couple minutes, she turns slowly and walks to the other side of the small meadow, against another embankment. The dirt's color is a perfect camouflage for her tawny coat. I follow her to the middle of the meadow as the drizzle progresses into a shower. This time I don't bother finding a tree for an umbrella.

As I stand a respectable distance from her, maybe twenty feet, it happens again. The doe, looking straight into my eyes, buckles her front legs and then her back legs.

And she lies down. My tears join the sky's. What magic is this? What mystery? What dream? I join her by sitting on a fallen tree in the middle of the meadow as the light wanes. Sitting there, looking at each other, then looking away at the vista beyond us, the blurry edges of disbelief begin to melt into a deep comfort of companionship. Without words, we engage in a conversation that isn't a lesson or an epitaph. It is simply a mutuality and a belonging that feels vaguely familiar.

After a while, I turn back to look at her, and she is gone. A rush of emotion floods from my heart up to my eyes, and I feel irrational betrayal. Why would she leave without saying goodbye? I get up quickly to walk toward where I'd seen her lying. Was all this beloved connection just my imagination?

Then I see her, six feet to the left of where I was looking before, camouflaged by the embankment behind her. Hidden only by my perception, the doe stands up, mirroring my confusion. We blink at each other for a moment, and I hear that same still, small voice I recognized as Christ within me. Or is it coming through this doe? "Even when you can't see me, I am always with you."

* * *

It happens a third time, the third day, with yet another doe. I kid you not. The rest of my human companions leave, and I decide to stay an extra day to have more time in this land.

I realize with this third doe that it is my turn to lie down before she does. My logical mind argues with itself:

"Well, if you lie down here, in the brush, then you can't see her at all. What good is this? Are you actually going a little crazy?" But my body does what it is told. After an extraordinarily long staring session, I lie down on crackling brown leaves, with sticks poking me in the back, staring up at the canopy of branches above me, and just . . . wait.

This wild doe, then, actually approaches *me*. I see her head peek over the brush around me. My breathing stops and my mind empties. This doe is curious about *me*. She comes to the edge of the small clearing where I am lying and gazes at me briefly before she starts casually chewing on some leaves. I start to cry again, in disbelief. When she turns to wander back to the large meadow, I feel the invitation to join her, and I nearly trip over myself following her. There, in the middle of a large meadow, only twenty feet or so in front of me, she looks me straight on, eyes to eyes, and lies down.

And we sit in the meadow together, just sit. Listening to the birds and the wind. I am not thinking about anything in particular. A deep resting, really. She settles into a deep rest, too, legs straight out, head lying on the ground. I lean back on the log near me. We watch the storm darken the sky little by little. The breeze turns cool. But we don't move, even with the thunder that begins booming closer to the lightning on the horizon. When the drizzle shifts into more of a deluge, the doe is not bothered or distressed. The rain is just part of life. A welcome part.

I wonder what it would it be like to stay here with her all day. But I am still a domesticated animal, unused to lounging outside in August rainstorms. My discomfort as the rain soaks through to my skin shakes me out of my reverie, and I get up to head back to my cabin. As I leave, she doesn't stand up. Rather, she nods toward me, or it seems like she does. I am safe. I am trusted. I feel it again, the strong sense that I belong. We share the same world.

Heading back along the trail, reality seems a little bent and sideways—so much so that I hardly flinch when I nearly bump into a moose. I instinctively hide behind a tree like one does when one sees the most gigantic animal one has ever seen in one's entire freaking life. As I wait for her to finish crossing the creek, I wonder if maybe I really am walking in a dream.

And then I feel the words rising up in me again, "I am with you always," and I remember where I've heard them before. God said them to Jacob in his dream. And Jacob, after awakening, exclaimed, "Yahweh is in this place, and I didn't know it."

* * *

Upon returning home, I felt compelled to find the meaning in my experience. Hesitant to read too much into it, I wondered at first if this is a common thing with deer in that region. But I could find nothing. I asked a member of the Ramapough Lenape Nation Deer Clan I had met at a climate conference in New York, and he only told me that this was some "powerful medicine," which I still don't really understand.

I knew I wanted to find a way to spend more time with deer. Searching the internet didn't help. It takes about four pages on Google before you can even locate a cabin to rent where deer live that doesn't have to do with wanting to kill them. My stomach started to churn with page after page of warlike depictions of bucks as enemies that men can destroy through Scent Crusher hunter's kits, body armor, gun magazines, and tactical clothing. Images on the packages for these things make it look like gear from *The Walking Dead* is needed to rid our country of the fearsome whitetail deer. (I apologize to readers who enjoy deer hunting and have logical arguments like subsistence hunting—which doesn't require militarized gear, by the way—and how deer have no natural enemies anymore since we killed most of them off. I get it. I still don't like it.)

Shifting my online search to avoid the hunters, I tried "meaning of deer," which turned up fun but not very meaningful things like "Deer represent caution and gentleness, reminding you to find shelter and to be gentle with yourself." Kind of like the "advice from a tree" posters you can buy from the bookstore. But I was not looking for cute little encouragements. I didn't want to feel *good*; I wanted to listen for the sacred meaning. I wanted to apprentice to these deer and honor this experience.

What was most helpful was just learning about deer themselves. I found out about a man named Joe Hutto, a wildlife biologist, who researched mule deer by living with them for years. He describes in intimate, respectful language how the deer accepted him into their herd. They eventually allowed him to touch them, lie down with them, and wander with them. He was even invited to see where their fawns were born. And the biggest compliment of all, he says, was when they simply ignored him. Even though the primary predator for this herd was the male human hunter, this herd came to know Joe as a trusted companion.

I learned through him that deer are a matriarchal species and that the female leaders do not lead with force or aggression. In fact, they do not engage with the normal squabbles from within the herd at all. That is how you can identify them. While the other deer flinch at any sound or movement, the leader mamas stay calm until they sense actual danger. When they do, they flee, and everyone else follows. There's some wisdom here for my journey, and for any who seek to be authentic leaders. This is a time when this energy of the matriarchal deer is needed.

Deer are prey who must be connected with their own fear for survival; yet they are not imprisoned by it. Most of their life is spent grazing, moving slowly, resting in meadows. They are always alert and watching, listening, feeling for potential threats, and respond instantly when necessary. But they don't live in a constant state of stress and fear. They rest easily and often.

In contrast, my body tries to handle fear by freezing or pretending I don't feel it. While that might sound less painful, it's actually an immense bondage. Fear is a necessary emotion, and by hiding from it, I'm actually aligning with it so closely that I find it difficult to just sit in a meadow for hours appreciating the rain. As with grief or anger or any emotion, fear, when fully expressed, makes space for calm to follow. This is something for me to pay attention to.

Like listening for the meaning in a dream, these kinds of encounters in the wilderness are actually not meant to be figured out—at least not in a direct, linear, cognitive kind of way. Glimpses of soul and spirit and wisdom are offered. We are invited to hold them, cherish perhaps, but loosely.

In *The Mabinogion*, a collection of early Welsh tales, does and stags appear as physical manifestations of the boundary between worlds: that liminal space between the known, familiar world and new, unmapped territory. Some say that following a deer is a way into the other-world or a sign that we are very close to its borders. I am beginning to learn that the otherworld is actually just our world alive, shimmering with divine presence. Waiting for our attention.

5
Restoring the Great Conversation

The heavens declare the abundance of God, the skies reveal
God's hands.
Day after day their speech flows out; night after night they
reveal knowledge.
There is no speech, and no language where their voice is
not heard.

—Psalm of David
11th century BCE

T he skies, the waters, the deer, the forests: these are
speaking all the time. We may have forgotten that we
have the capacity to understand their voices and to speak
with them, ask their advice, and seek their wisdom. Thomas
Berry lamented the losses we suffer—both us humans and
the rest of the world—in our separation: "We are talking
only to ourselves. We are not talking to the rivers, we are

not listening to the wind and stars. We have broken the great conversation."

The does I met in the Colorado mountains did not learn English, and I did not learn Mule Deer. But as we sat together in the rain, I felt welcomed back into a conversation I didn't even realize I was missing. They regarded me with an equality of being that humbled me. Berry suggested that restoring conversation with the rivers and deer and trees can actually repair the world. I don't think he was talking metaphorically—at least not completely. I think he was speaking to the inherent capacity we, as beings on Earth, have to actually engage in a conversation deeper than words, one which is going on all the time. And that conversation is what actually holds the web of life together.

When poet David Whyte was in the Galapagos Islands as a marine scientist, he said that his deep attentiveness to the landscape drew him into relationship with the beings he was studying. Those relationships opened him up to a deeper, wilder sense of self. In an *On Being* interview with Krista Tippett, Whyte shared, "I began to realize that my identity depended not upon any beliefs I had . . . [but] actually depended on how much attention I was paying to things that were other than myself—and that as you deepen this intentionality and this attention, you started to broaden and deepen your own sense of presence." By spending time with these beings, his own sense of presence and purpose shifted, and his calling as a poet was revealed within him. He now speaks of "the conversational nature of reality," which he says is the relationship that happens at the "frontier between what you think is you and what you think is not you."

Belden Lane, author of *The Great Conversation: Nature and the Care of the Soul*, invites us to find our way back into relationship with others from the natural world for the sake of the planet as well as our own spiritual and cultural revival. "We're surrounded by a world that talks, but we don't listen. We're part of a community engaged in a vast conversation, but we deny our role in it." Lane is a Presbyterian theology professor from a Jesuit university who is devoted to reconciling the divide between nature and spirituality. He shares his intimate story of learning to engage in long, loving conversations with Grandfather, an elder cottonwood tree who lives across the street from him in a park. He says he spends more time with Grandfather than with most of his friends: "For my part, 'Cottonwood' is a language I'm still struggling to acquire. I'm a slow learner. There's more to it than figuring out a new grammar and syntax. It's learning how to lean into bark, how to listen to leaves."

Learning how to converse with leaves and the long stares of mule deer is a spiritual practice that begins, as Lane says, with a sense of wonder. These moments are usually very small and humble moments of awe. Revelation can be like that. First you experience a numinous moment and then you need to find a frame for it and hang it up for others to see. Often these moments knock everything else off the walls, rearranging your worldview. Mystical conversations defy language. But *not* naming them leaves them without context, unable to grow into their meaning.

"By instrumentalizing nature, linguistically and operationally, we've largely stunned the earth out of wonder," writer Robert Macfarlane says in his book *Landmarks*. Terms like *natural resources, timber, private property, game animals*, and *livestock* desecrate the inherent value of non-human life. "Language is fundamental to the possibility of re-wonderment," Macfarlane reminds us, "for language does not just register experience, it produces it."

A language with gendered pronouns, for example, devalues every not-human being by calling them *it*. This linguistic practice is not only derived from a materialistic, disconnected, hierarchical culture; it helps to keep that culture in place. Author and botanist Robin Wall Kimmerer proposes a new "grammar of animacy," one that takes cues from her Anishinaabe language, where other species are "recognized not only as persons, but also as teachers who can inspire how we might live." The practice of regarding other species or elements as subjects—recognizing them as persons and teachers and kin—is contradictory to a culture invested in using others as objects. We need to develop a language of connectedness.

We have lost relational language for the natural world and lost part of our own souls along with it. In *Landmarks*, Macfarlane tells a story of how citizens of an island township called Lewis, on the Outer Hebrides of Scotland, saved their homeland by restoring intimate conversation with their landscape. The place is a bogland once referred to by the residents as a "nothing place" and as "unproductive wilderness." This kind of ambivalent language and attitude toward the land exposed it to exploitation. A gas and energy corporation called Amec showed up in 2004 proposing to build turbines across the moorland, which promised to decimate the biosystem.

Four residents knew they needed to do more than protest with conventional activist tactics. They launched a two-year campaign to inspire residents to restore intimacy with their land through specific storytelling. Restoration through *re-storying*. They called for the sharing of detailed and loving experiences that people had with particular places, encouraging them to tell stories, recall poems, create paintings and photographs, remember songs, recall lost words, map favorite hidden spots, and recount histories about particular places in their township.

The activists hoped to restore intimacy with the moor by encouraging particular conversations that reconnected the people and their place. And it worked. The townspeople collected and presented not statistics and petitions to their city council but stories and poems and songs as evidence of their restored relationship with the land. And the gas company's project was rejected. While other localities throughout Scotland had been unsuccessful in resisting corporate land developments, the citizens of Lewis were able to protect the integrity and health of the land and waters and creatures of their home by restoring conversation with them. The campaign revived the citizens' sense of kindred belonging to their place.

* * *

Most children begin life with an unconditional sense of kindred belonging to the natural world. When my son was a toddler, we would drive the back way out of Ojai on Creek Road toward Ventura, even though it took longer than taking the highway. He loved a short section of the winding road that went through a riparian area bursting with cottonwood and oak trees. Their branches reached for one another across the road, creating a tunnel that felt magical. I had started "talking the trees" to mediate a conversation happening between the trees and the small boy.

From his car seat in the back, Alec would shiver in giddy anticipation for the moment around the curve when we could see the tree tunnel. Beaming with joy, he would look up out the window and begin each conversation with "Hi Trees, it's Alec!" And I would answer in a low and wise voice, "Hello, Alec. We've been waiting for you." He would ask them about how they felt with the sun, update them on his life ("I'm going to get ice cream") and would show them his prized Matchbox cars.

When his sister, Olivia, was born and he was four years old, we had moved to Ventura and didn't have much use for Creek Road anymore. One day when she was a month or so new in the world, he asked if we could go and visit the trees. He wanted to show them his baby sister. "Hi Trees! It's Alec. Look! Baby Sister is here!"

Alec was a serious child. An observer. Few things lit up his eyes like the tree conversation. Once I made the mistake of being distracted when we approached the tree tunnel. He was indignant. "Mommy. Talk the trees!" Perhaps this early connection was a sign that he would be drawn deeply into relationship with the trees and the shore and the glaciers throughout his life.

Olivia, too, had a significant relationship with a particular avocado tree outside our house in Ventura, when she was around nine. She named him Leonardo and spent hours entangled with his limbs. Leonardo was her "alone space" where she could be invisible behind the thick layers of leaves, watching as neighbors walked right by her without knowing she was there. When her friends visited for playdates, Leonardo became their spy headquarters, complete with a pulley system for sending secret notes and avocados back and forth to one another.

Olivia is a girl whose imagination animates her. You can see the stories swimming through her body almost visibly. It shows up in the distant, enchanted look in her eyes and the mischievous half smile. Watching from our bedroom window, I could sometimes see her sitting under her tree, her head nodding and her mouth moving in affectionate conversation. Sharing heart-to-heart, she poured out the narrative of her life with the friend who could best keep secrets. Near the bottom of the massive tree's trunk was an indent that looked to Olivia like Leonardo's heart. There, in an act of sacred ritual, she carefully secured a glass heart-shaped pendant.

We only lived in that house for a couple years. We had to move because the chicken coop we built for our fluffy black chicken and white chicken, Fifi and Fo, was too close to the house on our tiny patio. Our neighbor complained to the city, who told us we had to get rid of the chickens. Instead, we moved.

Shortly before our final goodbye, when Olivia was at school, the landlord radically cut back the giant avocado tree. Beautiful Leonardo, with branches reaching down to embrace the ground and reaching up above the house like a multiarmed Kali dancer, was cut down to a trunk with nubby limbs sticking out. The heart pendant, he threw away. I had no words to comfort my traumatized and grieving daughter. A tree was not pruned that day; a friend was violated.

Olivia was forced to learn that sacred relationships and conversations with nonhuman beings like trees were not supported in this society. The separation was taught to her despite how hard I tried to help preserve her understanding of the tree's voice and value their relationship. This separation is ingrained in most of us. To restore conversation, authentic relationship with the rest of the natural world, an intentional unlearning is necessary. This work is necessarily countercultural.

* * *

As adults we continue to have enchanted experiences with the alive world, yet they are discounted by a rationalist culture as frivolous. Share a little about an encounter with a grasshopper whose gaze penetrated you, and people will smile awkwardly and change the subject. There is little context in our culture or in the Christian religion for these interspecies conversations, and they are often written off as little more than "woo-woo" spiritual stuff or sentimentalized as, "Aww, isn't that sweet?"

I've talked to many people over the past couple years who tell me, "I've had profound experiences connecting with animals and trees my whole life, and I held them to myself. I thought people wouldn't understand." And they may not. But some will. The experience of sacred conversation with others who are not human is actually a lot more common than you would think. I've noticed that most people have an intimate story with a particular tree. Or an ant they watched carrying a large leaf or an empty field where they would lie in the weeds and watch the clouds in the summer.

Try asking your friends this question: "Tell me about the land who raised you." I've found that nearly everyone knows how to answer it. And usually with animated enthusiasm, they share about the fields, the surf, the mud pies, the songs of meadowlarks who were as important to their early childhood as their families. It's like they were just waiting for someone to give them permission to regard these connections with nature as something important, even sacred.

* * *

Authentic conversation requires what writer Ursula K. Le Guin calls "a continuous intersubjectivity that goes both ways all the time." Conversation is not just a way to pass information back and forth like a computer. Actual living communication is about forming a relationship where listening and responding is not just the *medium* of connection; it *is* connection.

You can tell when you've just engaged in a true conversation. You feel seen and heard. You feel removed from routine events, renewed, refreshed, full of life, and open to possibilities. *Con* means "with," and *vertere* means "turn about." So the word *conversation* means "to change together": to turn and face each other with a sense of ongoing mutual growth, which is essentially the meaning of transformation. There is an intimacy involved and a risk. You are never the same after a real conversation. You turn and turn again and surrender what you used to think, and you end up creating something new with someone who is different from you. And you both end up just a little bit transformed.

A real dialogue is not possible when you treat the other as an object. Subjectivity is essential for conversations with cottonwood trees and deer and rivers. Anna Breytenbach, a professional and highly skilled animal communicator from South Africa, works with large sanctuaries harboring animals rescued from poachers, circuses, and other human abuses. She observes that wild animals can pick up human arrogance and will not engage with you if your posture is one of superiority. She demonstrates that if you approach them with reverence and respect—with a contemplative, quiet mind, and an open heart—they will often willingly engage with you, though not with words.

Even when we converse with other humans, only about 7 percent of what is communicated is verbal. Albert Mehrabian studied this in the 1960s and came up with what is now known as the Mehrabian Rule: 7-38-55 percent. Seven percent of communication is verbal; 38 percent is tone of voice; 55 percent is body language. And that is with other humans. Learning the language of leaves and deer and God, even, your intuition, embodied senses, and emotions guide you. Many fear that they will anthropomorphize the others. Yes, we are different beings, and we can make assumptions based on our own experiences just as we do when talking to other humans. But we actually have more in common with other beings than we commonly acknowledge. Fear of misunderstanding and appropriating only leads to avoiding relationship altogether.

In fact, quantum physicist David Bohm identified the specific moment when an encounter with an other turns into actual, relational conversation. Bohm discovered, through years of studying the dynamics of dialogue, that authentic conversation begins the moment you realize you are misunderstood! We often assume other people understand exactly what we are trying to say, but they never do. They can't. They are not you. This misunderstanding is actually essential to true conversation. It is the moment when you really start listening and allowing your own perspective to shift in response to the other. The back-and-forth, misunderstanding, clarifying, including what the other has said, and then adding to it—all this continues until a totally new understanding emerges for you both. Rather than disconnecting when we feel we aren't immediately understood, we can learn to see this moment of misunderstanding as the invitation into the experience of the other, which is a defining action of love. And something amazing happens: you both evolve.

This happens only if you can each freely listen to each other. Deeply. "Listening is not a reaction, it is a connection. Listening to a conversation or a story, we don't so much respond as join in—become part of the action," writes Le Guin. You are authentically interested in the other's different point of view, not proving your own as right. An authentic conversation asks you to be fully present, appreciate another's uniqueness, and discover what you have in common. You drop your old ideas for new ones that emerge through the iterative, back-and-forth interaction, a sacred reciprocity. You create meaning together, but that's not even the whole point. Conversation is the vehicle, the artery of connection, whether with a friend or a field of clover. Somewhere in the conversation, the content is almost not important anymore. The exchange itself creates and deepens relationship.

* * *

I often take a break from my desk to walk down the street to the little lagoon that is home to many shore birds. I like to set up my chair there just to listen in. I have an odd habit of counting them. This afternoon I'm drawn to the odd constellation of birds. Usually these early fall days, there are dozens of members from several species. But today, I'm noticing the singles. The mallard drake swims alone. A single bufflehead. A single adolescent seagull stays on this side of the lagoon with me. With all us singles. The drake quacks easily, as if an aside, speaking only to himself. A single crow. And a single goose.

A single goose is not good. Geese mate for life, and they are rarely alone. I've seen her here with her mate for weeks now, as they didn't fly south with the rest of the flock. For some reason, one of them wasn't up for it, so they stayed behind together.

Today this goose is alone, and inconsolable. I feel her grief as she slowly swims in circles around the lagoon with what sounds to my heart like weary, single-syllabled questions, "Where? Where? Where?" Paddling slowly toward me, looking through me, her calls are weak but relentless. A knot I didn't know was hiding there tightens in my throat. "Go? Go?" She finds her way up to the small, rocky beach, where there will soon be dozens of the black-necked beauties again. My heart is moved.

The compassion I feel penetrates my observer role. Her hoarse voice cracks open my own well-protected heart, unveiling my own loneliness. And I am able to release unwept tears and face the ways I have protected myself from intimate relationships since my children left the nest. I am grateful for the opportunity to feel my own hidden pain and connect with hers. In this conversation, I am reminded that all of us alive are deeply interwoven, not simply through the physical reality that we are dependent on the same waters and oxygen and gravity but through the reality of shared experiences of love, grief, and relationship.

I can't speak the goose's language, and she can't speak mine, but we are connected by something that I can participate in only when I slow down and take the time to approach her with reverence, appreciate her otherness, and allow the common bond between us to emerge. Her grief has opened my heart and unfolded my own grief. Feeling and then releasing emotion I had pushed aside, I can feel my heart open in places I did not remember were folded up.

Francis Weller, in his book on grief, says, "Grief and love are sisters, woven together from the beginning. Their kinship reminds us that there is no love that does not contain loss and no loss that is not a reminder of the love we carry for what we once held close." Only after we grieve can we be open again to love. The encounter, a simple connection with a goose, was an interaction of grace.

Every time we share our experiences with a goose or a deer or the every-year miracle of flowers coming up in spring—and acknowledge them with awe at the mystery of our interconnection—we take steps to repair the broken conversation.

* * *

Howard Thurman, the theologian and mystic who Congressman John Lewis called "the patron saint" of the civil rights movement, spoke with an eloquent language of connectedness. He is known for his oak tree prayers. "I could talk aloud to the oak tree and know that I was understood," Thurman wrote. In his intimate autobiography, *With Head and Heart*, he grounds his story of his social justice leadership in his deep spiritual intimacy with God and Earth. Thurman saw them not as separate relationships but as one, a connected and dynamic relationship with three parts: himself, God, and the world. Conversation between the three was natural, expected, and normative. "When I was young, I found more companionship in nature than

I did among people. The woods befriended me." Thurman's spirituality was deeply connected with the sacredness of Earth, rooted in wonder and awe, which is where all great conversations begin: "There were times when it seemed as if the earth and the river and the sky and I were one beat of the same pulse. It was a time of watching and waiting for what I did not know—yet I always knew. There would come a moment when beyond the single pulse beat there was a sense of Presence which seemed always to speak to me. My response to the sense of Presence always had the quality of personal communion. There was no voice. There was no image. There was no vision. There was God."

Thomas Berry proposed that "we will recover our sense of wonder and our sense of the sacred only if we appreciate the universe beyond ourselves as a revelatory experience of that numinous presence whence all things came into being. Indeed, the universe is the primary sacred reality. We become sacred by our participation in this more sublime dimension of the world about us."

As a spiritual director, I have walked with many people who share a long-standing and painful yearning for a direct and intimate relationship with God, with the holy. We *believe* that God loves us, but we know belief alone isn't enough. We want to *feel* the presence of the sacred with all of our senses and our emotions. We long to experience the sacred, and in that longing, forget to look outside our window and engage in conversation with a world that is already sacred, just waiting for our attention.

George Washington Carver was an agricultural inventor whose lifework could be defined by inventing new ways to help poor Black farmers, and their soil and plants, to thrive. He got it. Regarding his relationship with the many plants he nurtured throughout his life, he concluded, "If you love it enough, anything will talk to you." Conversation with plants and animals and trees and other beings in the living world is actually not much different from connecting respectfully and deeply with your partner or a friend, or prayer with God. You need to be attentive to your own inner chatter, your emotions, your assumptions about the other, setting them aside so you can be fully present. Then, you'll find you are fully present with yourself. And you'll begin to tap into a conversation going on all around you that is bigger than you. It's as big as God.

Repairing the great conversation means that we approach the world as alive, respecting that every individual—every single human, every single leaf, every single ant—is unique and has their own subjective reality. When we invest time and attention in connecting with others as sacred, as Thomas Berry said, "we become sacred." It's almost as if the connection between, the conversation itself, is how the sacred is manifested.

6
In the Beginning Was the Logos

In the beginning was the Logos.
And the Logos was with God.
And the Logos was God.
This was with God in the beginning.
All things came into being through this, and apart from this,
nothing came into being that has come into being. . . .
And the Logos became flesh, and dwelt among us.

—John the Evangelist
1st century CE

The idea of a divine indwelling at the center of the whole universe, with every unique part in conversation with the others, has many names. What Thich Nhat Hanh names the *web of interbeing* is aligned with what Robin Wall Kimmerer calls *sacred reciprocity*. David Whyte calls it the *conversational nature of reality*, and quantum scientist David Bohm uses the term *implicate order*. Martin Luther

King Jr. called it an *inescapable network of mutuality*, which he said was "tied in a single garment of destiny. Whatever affects one directly, affects all indirectly."

The ancient ancestors of Christianity called it *logos*.

Even with no connection to the Christian church, most people have heard the phrase that opens the fourth Gospel's story about Jesus: "In the beginning was the Word." John's Gospel has always been my favorite because of poetic statements like this. I love the cadence of the hymn, even in English. I preached on it several times throughout my career, usually connecting it with the opening of the Old Testament: "In the beginning God created the heavens and the earth." Jesus, I would say, was the incarnation, the enfleshment of this creative, alive-making *word of God*.

Poetically, *word* is fine. But my mind exploded—and my worldview too, along with my heart—when I began to investigate the 2,500-year history of this Greek word *logos*, translated in every Bible I've seen as *word*. I discovered that *logos* has a profound meaning that has been buried beneath a long history of patriarchy and mistranslation and empire. This word has the potential to completely reframe how we understand our interactions with Spirit, nature, and ourselves.

* * *

Logos was first used in a cosmological way by Heraclitus of Ephesus, a Greek philosopher in the fifth century BCE. He used the word *logos* to articulate a kind of intelligent life force embedded in and interconnecting all things, "a divine reason implicit in the cosmos, ordering it and giving it form and meaning."

Heraclitus was an irascible and fiercely independent figure, thinking outside the box before the boxes were even fully in place. One of the most revolutionary concepts he developed is the idea that all things are one. Scholars of wisdom in ancient Greece have heralded the significance of Heraclitus's ideas. Rhetoric scholar and philosopher Christopher Lyle Johnstone wrote, "As an intellectual and scientific development, the discovery of a unitary Nature was as revolutionary as the Hebrews' monotheism was in the history of ancient religions. This insight marks the invention of a *uni*verse, the conception of an indwelling unity behind the diversity in existing things."

Heraclitus developed *logos* to conceptualize the way the world functions as one collective, which he called the *kosmos*. *Logos* is the principle or power that shapes and creates all things, immanent and embedded in all that exists. He saw things not really as things, but as processes. *Logos*, he intuited, is the relationship between all things, holding them together. Later Greek philosophers would use the word *logos* to describe this relationship-between as a process of dialogue.

You can find the same concept in ancient Indian, Egyptian, Chinese, and Persian philosophical systems. New insights often emerge in different places, with different language, at around the same time. The Stoics, by 300 BCE, referred to *logos* as the "organizing, integrating, and energizing principle of the whole universe," working through all matter, including humans. In Chinese, *logos* is translated as *Tao (the Way)*: the principle "underlying the structures of the universe" that, while formless, gives life to "all shapes and forms of the material world." In Mandarin, *logos* is usually translated as *Dao*, a very similar cosmology that means going with the flow of the universe. It is a spiritual principle, but one that is deeply intertwined with ecological reality.

Logos also held an explicit sense that everything in nature is full of some kind of divine indwelling, worthy of reverence. *Logos* is similar to what biologists are revealing now about the way trees talk to one another and what quantum scientists have discovered at the center of molecules: not things, but relationships. *Logos* is about the divine relationship between all things. The system of their connection: conversation.

* * *

My sister, Valerie, and I had been geeking out on this idea of *logos* for several months. (We tend to get excited about the same things at the same time. Best friends are like that.) How quantum physicists and ancient philosophers were saying essentially the same thing. It was like the phenomenon I call "spotted frog." You do a report on spotted frogs you'd never heard of before and suddenly you see them mentioned everywhere. Familiarity bias. We saw *logos* everywhere!

Val sent me an article by historian Marjorie O'Rourke Boyle, which follows the historical story of *logos*. It's pretty academic, but as I sat curled up on my chair, with my laptop balanced on my knees and my journal on the end table, I could feel the connections unlocking possibilities in my head. Could my experience of conversation with the natural world have some roots in the Christ tradition?

Up until the fourth century, Boyle points out, theologians and bishops and translators consistently translated the Greek word *logos* into Latin, the language of the church, as *sermo*, which means not "word" but "conversation." *Sermo* indicates not a one-way sermon but a lively discourse, a dialogue, a manner of speaking back and forth: a *conversation*. A noun created from the root verb *serō*, which means to weave or join, *sermo* is the intimate living of life together, living among, familiarity, intimate conversation, the act of living with. *Sermo* was the Latin translation that best fit the meaning of *logos*.

The evangelist credited with writing the Gospel of John used this word and concept, familiar to the first-century citizens of the Roman Empire, as a culturally relevant way to talk about the idea of Christ. To position Jesus as more than a man crucified by the state, John sought to identify him with the *logos*: the divine indwelling "through [which] all things were made," an interconnected relationship underlying and holding together the whole universe.

"From Tertullian to Theodore de Beze," Boyle says, in order to include almost every second- and early third-century theologian, "extends a tradition of translating [*logos*] in Jn 1, 1 as *sermo*, a tradition now forgotten even by curators of antique words." Theologians and bishops who first studied the Gospel of John understood what the evangelist was trying to express: *logos* as a relational force, inherent in all things, holding together all things was an apt metaphor and description for Christ and for the role that Jesus fulfilled in embodying the Christ.

Richard Rohr, author of *The Universal Christ*, writes, "Jesus, for John, has become the universal Greek *Logos*, the divine principle of *Spirit acting as matter*—not a mere human person so much as a high-level statement about the shape of Reality. . . . Christ, as such, is not precisely a religious principle . . . [but] a life principle—the ubiquitous confluence of matter and spirit." We Christians get confused, thinking that Christ only refers to Jesus. But this opening of John clearly states that the Christ existed before the person Jesus. "Christ is not Jesus' last name, but the title for his life's purpose," writes Rohr.

Logos happens through relationship. This action of conversing—this intimate, abiding, turning to one another—is a sensual, living, flowing, never-ending relationship. It is the original primal relationship that has existed since the beginning and is reenacted in all matter and being. It is a relationship that all beings are invited into, and indeed, are already part of. Can we entertain that this relationship and action not only describes God's desire for humankind but is also the very being of God?

Reading Boyle's article, I felt something inside me instantly expand. The revelation hit me physically, like it does when an inner shift enters you as if from the outside: in my gut, my solar plexus, and my heart simultaneously. I stood up from my chair, disoriented, with my head swirling and my heart thumping in either fear or elation. I walked outside to see the stars and felt the stories rearrange inside me.

Christ as radical solidarity, as primal and ongoing relationship, as how life works. Christ as the Conversation between everyone and everything. This moment of insight changed everything for me. Replacing *Word* with *Conversation*, I said the whole passage—John 1:1–4, 14—out loud:

> In the beginning, was the Conversation, and the Conversation was with God, and the Conversation was God. This was with God in the beginning. All things came into being through this, and apart from this nothing came into being that has come into being. . . .
>
> And the Conversation became flesh and dwelt among us.

Just sit with that for a second. Read it, and now read it again. Did you feel it? Christ as an embodied, sensual, intimate reciprocity of giving and receiving; of listening and sharing vulnerably. Christ as that sacred Conversation that brings all things into being and links all things together. Christ as Love. In the beginning, the Conversation created all things, and through conversation, made all things new.

Entering into authentic conversation with others of all species, including our own, we participate in the story of Christ, our collective unfolding.

The Conversation is made flesh there.

The sacred is present there.

* * *

Quantum biologists and evolutionary scientists seem to concur with the Gospel of John: that at the center of all things is a deep conversation, a dynamic back-and-forth interpenetration and collaboration holding the system together. I am fascinated by quantum discoveries, but despite reading a few books, I don't pretend to really understand them. I'm just interested in the way truth shows up in different forms, using different languages.

Scientists looking for the ultimate building block of the universe once thought it was the atom. *Atom* means "that which cannot be further divided." Turns out, though, the atom can be further divided. But what's inside the atom looks less like a *thing* or even a noun at all. It is a process, like Heraclitus intuited—an evolving verb of continual relationship building. Scientists needed new language to describe what they were observing. Nouns like *protons* and *neutrons* and *quarks* were all right, but not entirely descriptive. What they really needed were verbs because what is "inside" an atom is a dynamic of relationality, radiating, changing into one another.

The English language, like other romantic languages including Latin and Greek, is oriented to entities (separate nouns) rather than relationships (verbs connecting them). Physicist Fritjof Capra attempted to describe the dilemma of articulation with languages that are heavily noun oriented, "A subatomic particle is not a thing but an interconnection between things, and these 'things,' in turn, are interconnections between other things." You never end up with "things"; you always end up with interconnections.

Physics is now considered a science of relationships rather than only a science of the structure of matter. Quantum physicists struggled with what ancient philosophers were also trying to articulate: at the core of all matter, life is animated by verbs of interconnection rather than nouns. *Relationship* is actually a more accurate way to describe the core operating action of reality. And a complex series of dynamic conversations hold all interrelating entities together. Biologist David George Haskell recognizes this in his book about the conversations and songs between trees: "The forest is not a collection of entities . . . [but] a place entirely made from strands of relationship."

The quantum scientists sought out the wisdom of Indigenous linguists to help them find language to describe what they were discovering. Most Indigenous languages and cultures are based in verbs. Robin Wall Kimmerer describes the difference between noun-based and verb-based systems this way: "English is a nounbased language, somehow appropriate to a culture so obsessed with things. Only 30 percent of English words are verbs, but in Potawatomi that proportion is 70 percent." Noun-based languages are concerned with describing the separate parts, the "things." In verb-based languages, the emphasis is on the processes and relationships between the things. A noun-based culture would see a thing (a tree, say) and might start to envision what can be made by using that tree: a table, a fence. Objectification of things is part of the structure of the language and, therefore, the culture. A verb-based culture, on the other hand, will see the relationship between the things.

It will see the interaction of the whole ecosystem: the tree relating with the wind and with the soil, and the water flowing through in relationship with the animals and the other plants, all dancing with the sun. Noun people will see the dancers on a stage. Verb people will see the dancing.

It is worth noting that many cultures, including Judaism and most Indigenous nations, consider the divine a verb, a relationship, rather than a noun. *Conversation* is a noun, yes, but it describes an active process of relationship, a sense of something that's more like a verb: "to dwell in a place, to live with, to abide, to pass one's life with." The action of conversing—turning to one another as intercourse and abode—is an intimate bond. Conversation is the original, primal relationship that has existed since the beginning and in which all beings participate.

And the Conversation was God: this suggests that God *is* the dynamic intimacy of relationship, a verb of back-and-forth, of connection, of Love that created everything and connects everything and moves everything forward. Everything—as in the whole cosmos! Not just humans but all things—before humans, including humans, but way larger than humans. This Conversation holds all things together, from the cosmos to nations to ecosystems to your own psyche. Practicing the presence of God is rooted in the very DNA of life. It's everything, working together.

The scientists watch it happen: atoms joining together in a sort of conversation with other atoms to become something new. Two hydrogen atoms unite with one oxygen atom and form a new entity: water. Two people attract and become a couple and create something new: little humans. A deer and a woman meet and the conversation between them, that energy of relating, creates a new way of approaching spirituality and nature. Is this not the work of Christ—to draw together opposites and create something new? Matter and spirit, male and female, darkness and light, me and you.

In the beginning was the Conversation. We are all part of an interconnected web of life, conversations going on at microscopic levels within our bodies. Conversations happening within family systems, within societal systems, within and between species, and within the biospheres where we all live. Conversations happening between the sun and the planet, between the galaxies and one another.

When we converse with each other, our conversation becomes a holy space of exchange: a space in which I release some of what I used to think and be in order to include you. And we both are changed. Conversation is expansive, unlimited, and reciprocal, requiring at least two particular beings to participate in an embodied relationship. Is this looking and listening and exchanging and changing what Jesus meant when he said, "Where two or three are gathered in my name, there I am in the middle of them"?

* * *

So why does every single modern version of the New Testament—no exception—translate the John 1 passage like this: "In the beginning was the Word"? Something happened in the fourth century that caused the Patriarchs to stop translating *logos* as *sermo* (conversation) and start translating it as *verbum*, or "word." It was an intentional decision that went against the grammatical and historical use of the word *logos*. And it mattered.

Language not only describes things; it also *produces* culture. A cultural lens that defines "successful life" in terms of nouns (things) will be concerned with an insatiable pursuit for more things. In that quest for owning more things, the ones with the most things are given the most power and thirst for more power. It's called empire. These are the ones who get to control the narrative and write the history. I'm not sure that a verb-based culture even thinks in terms of empire. But a noun-based culture creates it without even trying.

The Oxford Dictionary defines *empire* as a governing system that is focused on becoming and remaining the "single supreme authority." And it will destroy anything blocking its path. You may have noticed this. It gets expensive killing everyone who is already on the land that empire wants for itself, so religion serves as a handy tool to help empire control and assimilate the people. Excuse my sarcasm, but this reality makes me so angry. The more I've learned about this story, the more anger I feel—and the more determined I am to tell the story not told in seminary or in church or in most history books.

It is interesting that the person of Jesus of Nazareth showed up in history at a particularly volatile time of colonization. The noun people of the Roman Empire, speaking Greek, ruthlessly conquered many verb people, including the Hebrew-speaking Jews. This story is an ongoing trauma, replayed throughout the history of civilization and continuing today.

The New Testament was written in Greek, the common language of the Roman Empire in the Eastern Mediterranean. Greek is a language deeply rooted in nouns. The Greek-speaking, noun-oriented people of the Roman Empire were creating a new religion out of the stories of Jesus—passed down to them through the relational, verb-based Hebrew language and culture.

The tragic reality of the first four centuries following the life and death of Jesus is that the men in charge turned the revolutionary message of Jesus—*resisting* empire—into the very *religion of* empire. A book by Wes Howard-Brook, *Empire Baptized: How the Church Embraced What Jesus Rejected*, is a useful tool of reckoning with this. Howard-Brook explains that the early church, like the Roman Empire itself, was an urban phenomenon. Then, as now, those still connected with the land in the countryside were named barbarians, and their more nature-based religions, languages, and cultures were called vulgar. "The Romans relentlessly mined and logged everything in sight. The purpose of the earth was to produce food and other products that could become part of the imperial economy." They sought to domesticate both people and the earth from their wild state so that both could become raw material that could be shaped to serve "civilization." Clearly, not much has changed.

The early Jesus movement, born out of the Hebrew culture, was what Howard-Brook calls "a religion of creation":

a faith in which sacred encounters happen on Earth, in mountains, rivers, and wilderness. And it had pushed back against exploitation by empires for generations. Jewish prophets portrayed a lush and harmonious relationship with the land and animals. Yahweh sent people away from cities and into the wilderness again and again.

The Hebrew language is verb-based, and the worldview is focused accordingly on the verbs of relationship *between*. The Jewish people were less interested in defining the substance of God and more interested in how to relate to and please God. Yahweh, for them, was not a noun entity. God was a verb: God was *being* rather than *a* being. The only time the self-revealing "name" of Yahweh was offered to a human direct from the divine voice is captured in a mystical conversation with Moses and a burning blackberry bush. The sacred presence told Moses, "Take off your shoes because this is holy ground." This dirt up on this mountain? It's holy. Moses asked the name of this divine entity speaking to him from within the bush. The response—*'ehyeh 'ăšer 'ehyeh*—is a continuous active verb, not a noun. It is translated into English—a noun language—as "I AM WHO I AM," but a more verb-based way of translating this phrase would be something like "becoming which will be becoming," which doesn't sound much like a name at all. It's more like a description of an ongoing process of evolving, a present and changing existence (which sounds to me a lot like the ancient description of *logos*).

Anyway, Rome was about to collapse in the third century because the non-Roman, colonized peasants—in other words, the vast majority of the empire—were rebelling, and it was getting difficult to control them. The emperor found a way to "save" the empire by sharing leadership. Sounds like a cool idea—except that empires are all about single, supreme authority. Empires don't like sharing. So four different rulers were given four sections of the empire. It only took about thirty years for one of the ruler's sons, Constantine, who ruled a portion of the West, to kill everyone else and become sole emperor of the Roman Empire.

One of Constantine's first agenda items was to get the religion in order. He had attributed his military success to placing the symbol of the Christian religion on his soldiers' banners and shields. This led him to end persecution of Christians and eventually adopt the religion as his own (albeit on his deathbed.) But at that time, there were many different interpretations and expressions of Christianity throughout the kingdom, and that was causing conflict. Plus, a religion that asserts a single ruling identity for the deity would be helpful to remind folks that there was a new solo emperor too.

The fight was on for who was going to control the narrative of the newly legal church of the Roman Empire. Dissenting voices were shut down. And a war over the nouns of God was raging. The doctrine of the Trinity—a conceptualization of a single God with three parts—was forming through debates and fights and power trips.

So Constantine personally invited three hundred or so of the 1,800 bishops in the empire and escorted them, free of charge, to the imperial palace in Nicaea (now Bursa, Turkey, a lovely lakeside city). The bishops—all of them male, of course—were to come to agreement about the hotly debated hierarchy of the Godhead nouns, something their Hebrew predecessors never thought about. Defining the noun-ness of God "correctly" was an ongoing obsession of men with power.

The Nicene Creed was the result. These early church fathers—literally called the patriarchs—used language as a tool of dominance. From what I've read, the whole lot of them were power hungry, cloying for position and recognition, and they attacked one another mercilessly. These were the men who controlled the narrative. The Nicene Creed was meant to settle the God-noun argument and condemn any who dissented as heretics. And it's been used since then as a statement of orthodoxy, with slight adaptations, throughout history.

The Council of Nicaea didn't end the rivalry, though. For another sixty years, the debate over how to arrange the nouns of three entities to describe one God continued. People were excommunicated, exiled, and even killed over it. Finally the emperor Theodosius I ended the debate by imperial decree in 380: Nicene Christianity became the official state religion, complete with harsh condemnation of anyone with different ideas of what Christianity looked like, calling them "mad men" and persecuting them with a "divine authority." The pope commissioned a revised set of Old Latin gospels to be used authoritatively by the Roman Catholic Church. These were called the Vulgate, meaning "for the commoners," which is ironic because the commoners didn't read Latin—only the priests did.

In this sanctioned Vulgate version of the New Testament, the decision was made to use *verbum* (word) to translate *logos* for the opening hymn of John 1. *Verbum* means just one single vocable, the smallest fragment of language that has meaning: a single word. While it doesn't make grammatical, contextual, or historical sense, it does make a point. Word (*verbum*) fit the objective of the "single supreme authority" of the now official Holy Roman Empire Church.

After all, allowing Conversation (*sermo*) to define the essence of Christ could encourage those dissenting voices to be heard. No. They had been effectively shut down. *Word* was better. No back-and-forth, no room for dissent, no changes. Just the one and only Word, the last word, the capital-W Word. The inarguable Word, the end-of-discussion Word, the everyone-else's-word-is-heresy Word. The hierarchy chooses *Word*, and so it remains *Word*.

End of conversation.

* * *

This translation decision went unquestioned for more than one thousand years, and the debate about *logos* was largely forgotten. But then a man in the sixteenth century—a contemporary of church reformers like Martin Luther and John Calvin—translated the book of John and the rest of the New Testament directly from the original Greek documents. He was the first to do so.

Erasmus of Rotterdam, a committed Catholic, didn't side theologically with the reformers like Luther and Calvin, but he dared to challenge the Vulgate, the official Roman Catholic translation. Fiercely dedicated to academic scholarship, Erasmus tried to stay as close to the original intent of the authors as possible. His stated objective was to make the New Testament available to the actual commoners, even (gasp!) women.

So in 1516 Erasmus ignited a huge controversy when he released the second of his Latin New Testament texts after he discovered that *Logos* didn't mean *Word* (*verbum*) at all. It meant *Conversation* (*sermo*). So he changed it. "In the beginning," the translation in English would be, "the Conversation was God."

As you can imagine, the institution of the Holy Empire freaked out. Some Protestant Reformers, including Calvin and Zwingli and Luther, cheered his efforts. But many more reviled him for it. Marjorie O'Rourke Boyle says that Erasmus "spent more ink defending his translation of logos" than he did penning translations of the entire Bible, which he did twenty-five times during his life. Erasmus relentlessly defended his use of *sermo* (conversation): "*Sermo* . . . more perfectly explains why the evangelist wrote [*logos*], because among Latin-speaking men *verbum* does not express speech as a whole, but one particular saying."

While Erasmus was still alive, William Tyndale published an English version of the Bible relying on Erasmus' text. But there was one very intentional exception: *logos* was still translated *verbum*, or Word. Apparently the Protestants were no more interested in relinquishing authoritative control than the Catholics were.

Ten years after Erasmus's death, the Catholic Church convened the Council of Trent to condemn the Protestants and the work of Erasmus too. They ordered all copies of

Erasmus's translation to be burned, and they issued an edict that the only True Word of God was the Vulgate, the official and approved biblical text of the one and only True Church.

Fifty years later, the Vulgate was revised, quietly integrating several of Erasmus's corrections, with the obvious and intentional exception of *logos*. A God who is Conversation is still a threat to the Word of Authority of the church.

In the beginning was the Word. Just one Word. Mine, not yours.

* * *

God as the Patriarch. Christ as the Lord. God as the King. Christ as the One and Only Word. These are all metaphors or images created by people (well, men) at particular times in history to define relationship with sacred reality. These are metaphors that made sense to people who were ruled by violent, imperial monarchs—people who depended on the whims of lords and property owners for their survival. These metaphors also conveniently helped those in charge to legitimate and enforce their power.

Ecotheologian Sallie McFague calls on us to construct new images and metaphors that are relevant to our lives and time in history. For us, living in this century, metaphors for God must somehow experiment with metaphors other than the royalist, triumphalist images, which are clearly inappropriate. They must, she insists, express the ecological interdependencies of life. McFague suggests a metaphor of Earth as God's body. "The model of the world as God's body encourages holistic attitudes of responsibility for and care of the vulnerable and oppressed; it is nonhierarchical and acts through persuasion and attraction; it has a great deal to say about the body and nature." She argues that new metaphors like this can help us take seriously the sacred nature of all bodies, both human and more than human.

I agree. And I offer another relevant metaphor for our time, yet rooted in a forgotten tradition: Christ as Conversation. Christ as Conversation says to me that the oak tree and that deer in the meadow are not God. And I'm not God. But we both carry the Christ, the Logos, the Tao, the spark of divine love within us. And the conversation between us: *that* is the manifestation of the sacred, moving forward the evolving kin-dom of grace. The wild Christ.

Using the word and metaphor of *conversation* rather than *word* is the most grammatically, contextually, and emotionally accurate translation of this pivotal Scripture. This version has been suppressed by a 2,500-year-long history of patriarchy. Reviving it is an act of resistance.

Jesus as the Christ embodies that in-between presence between the Creator and the created. Between the transcendent and the incarnated. But not just Jesus. All of us. Even the trees and the microbes and the stars are made and imbued with and held together by Conversation. Christ is dynamic, abundant relationship, a cacophony of interrelated connections navigated by conversation. Christ is the opposite, in fact, of a static word, a single utterance controlled by powerful men.

Imagine what one word change could do. Benjamin Lee Whorf, the Yale linguist who suggested in the 1940s that our language can determine our experience of life, knew that "a change in language can transform our appreciation of the Cosmos."

Imagine what could happen if a spirituality by the Word of authorities transitioned into a spirituality guided by Conversation with a living, interconnected world.

If the imperial agenda of the powerful—by co-opting a religion for its own purposes—can have a centuries-long impact of violence and control, what would a wild Christ—a Conversation who is the intermediary of love between all things, whose divine presence connects wild deer with my own wild soul—evoke in our world? Is it possible to imagine the worldview of kingdoms and empires transforming into a worldview of kin-dom and compassion? Imagine how different life would be right now if Christianity could become a place for sacred conversation: a place to explore possibilities and express doubts and disagree and encourage voices on the edges. Imagine the church honoring sacred conversation by lifting up the voices shut down by empire. Imagine the reconciling role the church could offer in bringing together opposite forces to remember that we are all interconnected.

Wild spirituality is an opportunity to reorient our relationship with the whole world through a wild Christ that existed before words and churches and empires. It is an act of resistance against the attempts to sever human participation from the whole system of life. Spiritual practices that reconnect us in conversation with the sacred world are the underground mycelium of church of the wild.

7

Courtship of the Particular

Love all God's creation, the whole and every grain of sand
  in it. Love every leaf,
every ray of light. Love the animals, love the plants, love
  everything.
If you love everything, you will perceive the divine mystery
  in things. . . .
When you are left alone, pray. Love to throw yourself on the
  earth and kiss it.
Kiss the earth and love it with an unceasing, consuming love.
  —Fyodor Dostoevsky, *The Brothers Karamazov*
                                    19th century CE

Heart-opening, transformational conversation often happens in small moments: an unexpected gasp of awe as colors shine more vividly and you can almost see the threads of the web connecting you; at least you can feel them. For me, it began with quiet invitations from mule deer to lie down in the rain. But that was only the invitation. These encounters are invitations to fall in love. Relationship is where the holy dwells.

You can "love the earth" by taking care of it: by getting involved with advocacy campaigns to remove dams and protect forests, by living simply and adding nutrients to the soil, by limiting fossil fuels and eating local foods. And I hope we all do. All of us need to make significant changes that may feel, at first, like sacrifices, yet in the end are only the surrender of privileges that were never ours in the first place.

But falling in love with Earth? That's different. First of all, it's a bit of a misnomer. You don't fall in love with Earth; she's too big. You are allured to pay attention and enter into conversation with a particular being, a particular place. And then, through fidelity and time and a thousand small acts of kindness and reciprocal giving and receiving, you fall in love. Through that particular, deepening relationship, a portal is opened and your heart is expanded to love the whole.

To quote farmer and poet Wendell Berry, "People exploit what they have merely concluded to be of value, but they defend what they love. To defend what we love we need a particularizing language, for we love what we particularly know."

This is a courtship of the particular. Of the many others in the world, some—or maybe just one—will choose you. Pursue you, even. We love *all* by authentically loving the one or the few who are near us: those who give themselves to us to whom we open our hearts and love back. To regard a wild one as a sacred other, one who has her own wisdom and relationships and concerns beyond our encounters with her—this is entering into conversation as a practice of love, which is participation in the presence of the sacred, of Christ.

* * *

I tried to connect with wild deer everywhere I went. I really did. For years after my "doe experience," whenever I would see a small herd near the road, I'd stop my car and try and catch up with them. I'd hike where I knew they had been seen. But they could sniff my earnestness and earnestly avoided me.

At subsequent Seminary of the Wild programs, everyone—no exaggeration—everyone but me would engage with deer. Even on my vision fast a couple years later, during which I spent three days solo in mule deer country, the only doe-like presence I encountered were the bones of one of their kin, whitened by years of exposure. I kept the bones near me, in my prayer circle. They held meaning for me, but I couldn't help but feeling disappointed. Like all kinds of falling in love, it doesn't work to try and force a relationship. Eventually I gave up. I decided that the experience I had was a gift not to be repeated and let it rest in the back corners of my mind.

Meanwhile, I made a move from Ojai, California, to Bellingham, Washington. I had moved many times during my life, always for a job or a landlord's whim or for family reasons. But for the first time, with my kids launched in college and beyond, I made a move specifically for a place.

I was evacuated from my home when the Thomas fire consumed 280,000 acres around Ojai. In 2017, it was the largest wildfire in recorded California history. (Though every year since then, the wildfire record has been broken more and more dramatically.) When I left in a rush that day, I had no idea that I'd end up driving all the way to Washington, where my son lives, because none of my friends in California could take me and my two cats in.

The first time I drove into Bellingham, driving north from the metropolis of Seattle, past megasuburbs that turned into agricultural land, I drove around a curve and the land transformed into forest. Thick evergreen trees lean into I-5 from both sides, like they are peeking over one another to see you driving by. The air changed, even inside my car, and I felt a weight lift from my shoulders, physically. I felt my lungs fully inflate. A disoriented familiarity told me, irrationally, that this place was calling me home. The cedar trees and the Salish Sea, the ferns and migrating swans, the bay, the rain and wind beckoned me. I understood why my son had settled in the Pacific Northwest. My Ojai house survived the fire, but I returned only to pack up and make the move toward the rainy north.

After my friends who helped me move had gone home, I looked around at the boxes that had been in storage for five years and realized that this was the first time I'd lived alone for thirty years. What gratitude that I was able to rent this remarkable maroon two-story house, built in 1904 and restored just enough that the many windows were double paned. Giddy with a taste of the freedom everyone promised would come after the grief of the empty nest, I grabbed the keys to the moving truck to return it before the rental place closed.

I ran out the front door onto a dark porch. And I nearly tripped over the doe who was lying down at the bottom of the steps.

*　*　*

I think it's probably true that love waits until you give up trying. Song of Solomon's refrain is positioned as a warning, but it might just as well be a statement of how reality works: "Do not arouse or awaken love / until it so desires." You can't force it. I don't know why it works that way, but it does. I also can't explain to you how it is that I know that the deer were calling me to Washington, even though I didn't actively know it until I got here. The does I met in Colorado were the messengers calling me to pay attention. The deer who live in the neighborhoods of Bellingham drew me into relationship.

Appreciating nature is important, but it isn't enough. Working to protect nature is good, but it isn't enough. Writing a book about nature isn't enough. The only way to grasp the conversation of sacred connection is to move beyond caring and risk falling in love. Belden Lane, in *The Great Conversation*, remarks that "only in risking ourselves to wind and fire, cave and tree, birdsong and wolf-cry can we grasp the language of glory whispered through it all." He's describing a fully embodied and personal contact, which "demand[s] our falling in love—crazy, self-abandoning love—in giving ourselves to wild things."

I could hardly believe that deer, whom I'd been relentlessly pursuing over the past five years, were now casually wandering into my yard. This neighborhood was built where a forest used to be. The black-tailed deer, a subspecies of the mule deer I met in Colorado, have adapted to the human development that took over their habitat, and a few families of does and their offspring live their whole lives within three miles of my house. I speak blessings over them when I see them on my walks, "May you find enough food and a safe place to sleep and protection from cars and dogs." But it wasn't until I met a particular doe that I learned what it felt like to fall in love with a being from another species. I named her Mary.

Wild animals choose to be seen by you, not the other way around. Mary chose me. The first time I saw her, I had an apple and held out a slice to her, as a gesture of offering. I was surprised and thrilled when she walked straight up to me and took it from my hand, something she never did again.

I recognize Mary not only because she is the only deer in the neighborhood who walks toward me when she sees me but because I know her face so well. I've spent an aggregate of many hours studying her face. Her left ear has a series of four small tears, as if they were cut neatly by scissors. And the right ear has a small rectangle missing on the edge. I always wonder what happened.

It is her eye, though, that I recognize, even from a distance. Mary has a scar leading from just above her mouth up to the front corner of her right eye. The eyeball is deflated a little. It isn't as round and tight as her other eye. She stands so close to me, sometimes as close as one or two feet, that I can examine the dark pupils, wide and oval, only slightly darker than her brown irises. She looks at me straight on, chewing the apples. It makes me laugh; she is so serious about it. She intensely examines me and is probably making note of the recognizable features in my face as well.

Now I can finish a piece of art I started a couple years ago—it is part of a series of Madonna and Child paintings that I've been creating throughout my life. I began the series when my daughter was an infant. In the painting, Mary is looking down at Jesus, nursing. Surrounding them are listed all the monastic prayer times—Vespers, Lauds, Matins—and pages torn from my *Book of Common Prayer*, "ordinary time." I had noticed that the monastics prayed every three hours, which is precisely when my babies needed to be nursed. My nursing time was always a contemplative time for me. Entitled *Some Pray with Psalms, Some Pray with Milk*, the painting helped me transition to a different rhythm of prayer marked by the demands and gifts of motherhood.

Another in the series is a Black Madonna, with her baby Jesus strapped to her back, looking straight at the viewer. It had always bothered me that all the icons of Mary show her looking demurely aside. No way. Mary, mother of

Jesus, was seriously fierce. So my Black Madonna shows her and baby Jesus looking straight out of the painting into your eyes.

In this most recent painting, Mary is a deer. Below her golden halo, she is lying down in a field, and baby Jesus is the fawn standing next to her, with his golden radiant disc. Painting this was a way to for me to deepen into this understanding—that all beings are a reenactment of the divine incarnation. The painting had been sitting unfinished for two years. I just couldn't get Mary's eyes right.

Once I met Mary, the black-tailed deer who comes to my house, I realized the painting could not be finished because I was not painting a face of an actual unique being. I had been trying to paint "a deer." But now that I have the actual beloved face of this particular deer, I have pulled out the canvas to capture her particular features and essence in the painting.

* * *

Today as I write this, I can see Mary is particularly hungry and seems tired. This is her third visit today, and I haven't seen her for over a week. Her trusting eyes reveal weariness. Her deerlike readiness to flee at any sudden or fast movement is a bit dulled. I cut two apples for her and she eats them slowly.

It is a balmy late spring evening, and the sun, which doesn't set till nearly nine o'clock, is still bright, but the colors of the yard are soft. The gentleness of the deer's presence is mirrored by the way the breeze moves softly through the trees, releasing the last of the white blossoms from the cherry tree. I grab a glass of wine to sit on the porch to watch her. She is grazing slowly through the yard, and I pick up my phone absentmindedly. How easy it is to distract myself from the present, even during a sacred moment like this.

But Mary's gaze, standing only about ten feet from my chair on the porch, draws me tenderly back into a state of presence. Satisfied with the leaves and dandelions in my yard, Mary looks straight at me and buckles first her front legs, then her back legs, and she lies down in the grass near me. This echoing moment calls me into full attentiveness, and I lay aside my phone completely.

I'm not as good at contemplation as Mary is. But she asks nothing less of me. Can I sit here with her, present and open and calm, even as she is? Mindful of the birds, the squirrels, the air. Without agenda or doing. Just being. Once I surrender, the contemplative presence is much easier and more natural than the meditation and prayer practices I struggled to get right throughout my life. I can feel my shoulders release, and I take a long breath, allowing the grace of this moment to sink in.

Little by little, Mary relaxes more until she is lying with all four legs stretched out, just like the deer in the meadow five years earlier. And I can see now that she's just given birth. Her udder is swollen and her nipples erect. I can still see some birthing goo she's trying to lick clean.

I remember those first few hours after giving birth to my two children. Liminal and surreal. Every color heightened by the strong presence of love yet blurred by the exhaustion. Holding and nursing their pink warm bodies, just moments after their ridiculously painful births, really did make the memory of the pain disappear. I'd been told this happens by the midwives. During labor, however, I was convinced they'd lied to me. I told them that I'd *never* forget this pain, ever. But bodies are made to forget. Or we'd never have more than one child, ever.

My babies were born at home and stayed with me nearly every moment for several years. Slings, attachment parenting, family bed—the whole nine yards. I'd be freaking out if I was separated from my babies on the day of their birth. But Mary appears unhurried to get back to her infants, who are safely hidden in tall weeds in a neighbor's neglected yard. I've read that in the first three weeks of the fawns' lives, their mother leaves them in their safe nest for up to eight hours at a time while she wanders and grazes. They don't have any scent the first few days, so a dog can walk right by them and not notice. Until the babies can run quickly enough to evade predators, their best protection is to stay hidden while their mother gets her own nourishment and can come back to nurse them. So even while they are growing, the little ones need safe places to rest for hours at a time.

I try to see any tension in her, any anxiety about leaving her vulnerable newborns alone. But I sense no trace of my anxiety in her. She is in no hurry. No rushing. No stress. We sit together for at least an hour. I sip my chardonnay. She chews her cud.

* * *

The next day, when Mary brings her twin infants to meet me, I'm so excited I can't even think straight. Sitting at my desk that looks out to the garden, I see two fuzzy, spotted, fragile, miniature creatures prancing behind their mama. My nervous system goes into hyper mode and I lose all sense of protocol, bursting out the door with my camera and congratulations. And I totally spook the tiny newborns, causing cautious mama to leave immediately.

I need to leave them alone and respect the liminal space of those early days of a new family. I realize I regarded them only through my own excitement, insensitive to their needs. But Mary forgives me and returns almost every day, sometimes with her fawns.

Every time I see her I drop everything, interrupt Zoom meetings, and leave participles dangling in order to cut an apple into fourths. I force myself to calm my mind and slow my pulse before opening the door slowly and quietly. As I offer Mary gifts of apples, she offers me the gift of her presence and the privilege of watching her tiny, miraculous fawns prance around the picnic table.

After about two weeks, one of Mary's twins is gone. I assume their birth nest is no longer safe. I can feel Mary's grief in her gaze. The remaining fawn, whom I named Marta, stays close to her. But since she is still small and fragile and needs to spend most of the days resting while her mother grazes, she needs a particularly safe place to hide.

My desk is placed in the corner of my kitchen. Two large windows allow me to look out onto a little greenhouse shed that a former tenant built. Behind that is a small, neglected garden, fenced in on three sides and lush with green weeds. I've only just started to clear away the giant comfrey plant taking it over. Looking out from my desk one morning, I see baby Marta, curled up asleep.

It becomes a daily routine. Mary stops for a couple apples, and Marta hops to her spot in the garden, paws at the ground a bit, buckles her legs and lies down. Mary then sets off to do her important grazing in the neighborhood and returns several hours later. It doesn't seem possible, but Mary has apparently decided that I am a worthy fawn sitter.

Marta naps here all morning. Every couple hours she gets up to look around for her mother. She nibbles at the leaves she likes best and walks up to me, looking up to my eyes, and then down to the ground, up and then down. It's her way of asking for more of those apple slices. The trash truck, in all its loudness, comes by, and Marta runs in terror, as she is created to do, to the edge of the yard. She stands in taut attention watching, slowly remembering that she's seen this loudness before. Marta locks eyes with me. I trust what I feel, and I know she is looking to me for assurance. As I whisper words of comfort and affirmation, her eyes soften and calm, her body relaxes, and she slowly lifts her back leg to scratch her delicate chin. I'm filled with so much love I can't hold back the tears. How do creatures this exquisitely vulnerable survive in a domesticated human environment like my neighborhood?

I can't help but project my own mothering worries onto them. I hear the parallel narratives in my head echoing my own experience of pulling away from my kids, a slow, necessary, and painful separation we quaintly call the empty nest. As Mary leaves Marta alone for longer and longer periods of time, I feel my mothering hormones flaring into anxious wonderings at deer family values. Maybe Mary is a particularly bad mom and has forgotten about her? Maybe Mary is injured? Maybe she has gotten into a collision with a vehicle, which claims the lives of five thousand deer in Washington annually. Maybe a dog has chased her or a cranky neighbor poisoned her? It's official: I've become a neurotic deer lady.

But Mary has always returned. She comes up to my window and stares at me, hoping for more apples. Always she is hoping for more—like my old lab, Molly, who would gulp with desperation and Jedi-stare at me with an occasional nod of her eyebrows down to the cookie I was eating.

My son suggested that perhaps Mary is not just stopping by for apple treats. "Did you ever think she's just coming to see you?" He may be right because she comes to visit and accepts my gift of apples, cut up in fourths, even when the apple trees in the neighborhood are prolifically providing her primary food source.

Why is it so difficult to believe that the wild ones we love actually love us back?

I love Mary. But does she love me? Robin Wall Kimmerer, in *Braiding Sweetgrass*, writes, "Knowing that you love the earth changes you, activates you to defend and protect and celebrate. But when you feel that the earth loves you in return, that feeling transforms the relationship from a one-way street into a sacred bond."

To disbelieve that Mary loves me is to diminish that sacred bond. That is not love. To approach her from a dominant position and disregard her innate intelligence, beauty, compassion, and capacity to love is to break the conversation. To assume that I am the only one responsible for this sense of love—without the generosity to respect her beingness as inherently valued—is to refuse the presence of Christ. I have no choice but to believe what my body and soul already feel: she does love me back.

When asking this same question, Kimmerer comes to this exultant conclusion: "I knew it with a certainty as warm and clear as the September sunshine. The land loves us back. She loves us with beans and tomatoes, with roasting ears and blackberries and birdsongs. By a shower of gifts and a heavy rain of lessons. She provides for us and teaches us to provide for ourselves. That's what good mothers do."

* * *

Craig Foster, filmmaker and the human subject of the astonishing documentary *My Octopus Teacher*, was snorkeling in the mysterious wilds of the ocean near his home in South Africa when he met a common octopus. Charmed, he decided to return and visit her every day. Eventually, one day, the shy solitary being chose to breach the species barrier we imagine is there and tentatively touched him with one of her tentacles. What unfolded was a stunning, heartbreaking love story. Foster unapologetically uses language of "falling in love" that breaks down the viewer's barriers. By the end of the film, you can't help but love this odd creature and understand the relationship as a courtship that grew into a transformative relationship.

'The encounter with the particular invites us into a relationship. And the relationship awakens something within us, inviting the everyday fidelity of just being there for one another, which is the real transformation of love. Eventually, Craig founded a nonprofit organization dedicated to protecting the bay where he visited his beloved octopus teacher every day until she died. This is part of love too. Love is more than an emotion; it is a response to the gift of life that begins with and then expands beyond the particular.

"You can only protect what you love. You only love what you know. You only know what you are in deep relationship with." This quote is my version of . . . hmm. Honestly, I cannot tell who first said it because it's become anthologized and restated so many times that it's hard to tell where it began. Like all great truths, these words come into consciousness through many channels and cannot be trademarked. The quotation has been attributed on Pinterest to Jacques Cousteau. And maybe he did say it once, but I don't think he was the first to coin it. Maybe it was Baba Dioum, a Senegalese forester who wrote in a UN paper in 1968, "In the end, we will conserve only what we love, we will love only what we understand, and we will understand only what we are taught." Others like Richard Louv, author of *The Nature Principle*, modified it to say, "We cannot protect something we do not love, we cannot love what we do not know, and we cannot know what we do not see. Or hear. Or sense." Cornel West, Harvard professor and prominent activist and intellectual, adapts it to racial justice work. "You can't lead the people if you don't love the people. You can't save the people if you don't serve the people."

Once you fall in love with a particular other—a shoreline, a tree, a meadow, a particular deer or dog or bay—it is not such a difficult thing to come up with new ways to protect and care for and adjust your lifestyle around the well-being of these others. These others become part of you. Defending them becomes defending your own family.

It's not much different from falling in love with your intimate partner or child. Once you are in loving relationship, you no longer have to campaign for every single one of your needs. It is a commitment of sacred reciprocity that deepens with time and much forgiveness because we are all broken. You begin to learn their needs and their desires and you anticipate them and learn surprising new ways to please them. They are, in turn, energized in giving you what you need simply because they love you.

* * *

In 2016, I went to Standing Rock. I drove 1,600 miles, stopping to watch the stars from underneath layers of blankets in the Wyoming snow, so I could join twenty thousand others to protect one river with the people who love her. The water protectors were opposing the Dakota Access Pipeline, which was pushing its way through the Standing Rock Sioux reservation land without permission or a legally necessary environmental impact report. The pipeline posed a serious risk to the people as well as to the water herself. The leaders of the Sioux Nation had been opposing the pipeline for years, but in 2016, a series of protest encampments drew the attention of the world.

Defending a river for her inherently sacred existence was not the typical call to action of the white liberal environmental movement, much less the practice of any white religious community I knew. While North Dakota law enforcement officials and private armed guards hired by the energy corporation responded to the protests with violence and arrests, Indigenous elders grounded the dramatic nonviolent confrontations in prayer.

One evening is seared into my memory. A large group of us are gathered around the sacred fire, and an Apache medicine man tells us how he gave up the ways of the Green Frog, driven by money and television sets, when he was twenty-seven. He found happiness again, he says, when he returned to the ways of his ancestors, to the ways of the Creator. As our hearts open and the rest of us consider how we, too, are still in the clutches of the Green Frog, the Apache medicine man tells us that he adopted us. All of us: the warriors, the hippies, the tribes they once opposed, even the white eyes who betrayed them. Even me. He calls us his relatives.

The next day, the Native elders pray at the barricade in blizzard winds. I feel proud to be standing shoulder to shoulder among those the medicine man reminds me are my kin. For two hours in the below-zero windchill, we chant "*Mni wiconi, mni wiconi, mni wiconi!*" as if the prayer itself—"Water is life!"—has the power to change the world. I stand with Sioux elders, Lakota and Hopi, lawyers, housewives, priests, lovers, grandmas who are always escorted to the front of the food lines, veterans from wars that healed them from warring. A mother from Minnesota; a reporter from Norway; burning men who met at Burning Man; a group of Black youth calling for nothing less than revolution; white students, full of hope that they, too, might be arrested; and a doctor who discovered an enzyme that predicts neonatal difficulties. Gazing at the miles-long line of people singing in the face of the armed police on the other side of the bridge, I recognize, as the tears piercing my eyes turn to ice: I've never felt more alive.

When the decision comes down the next morning, the Sioux elders meet at the sacred fire. The environmental impact report, Chief Looking Horse reads, has been ordered by the Obama administration. It's the decision they've been fighting for, the one that will offer the river a chance. Billows of celebration erupt, whooping and hugging and flag waving ripples through acres of the twenty thousand.

I am standing close to the elders, though, and something else is happening. The elders, after reading the news, begin planning. Among them there is no whooping or high fives. No victory fists lifted in the air. There is no delay, not even a beat between words. The elders begin planning not a congratulatory party or a feast but . . . a forgiveness ceremony.

Is it imaginable that a mysterious and yet powerful movement might be led by those who have never lost their sacred connection from Earth? May we open our ears and our hearts and, with humility, learn from these elders.

The strategy? Prayer.

The organizing structure? Prayer.

The tactics? Prayer.

The call to action? Prayer.

The march to the barricades? Prayer.

The response to violence? Prayer.

The response to victory? Prayer.

The response to fear? Prayer.

The response to ongoing betrayal, injustice, infuriation? Prayer.

The celebration? Forgiveness.

Is it possible to change the world by love alone? I believe the Apache medicine man when he says that he has adopted us. We are already kin. So, yes. I believe that only love can prevail against the unraveling we are facing.

8
Love Is as Strong as Death

A charitable heart . . . is a heart which is burning with love
for the whole of creation. . . . He who has such a heart
cannot see or call to mind a creature
without his eyes being filled with tears by reason of the
immense compassion
which seizes his heart; a heart which is softened and can
no longer bear
to see or learn from others of any suffering, even the smallest
pain, being inflicted upon a creature.
— Saint Isaac the Syrian, *Mystic Treatises*
7th century CE

There is a kinetic energy in the air this evening. The sun is glowing on the trees in the late afternoon so that everything looks like a Maxfield Parrish painting. But the glow is also coming from some kind of energy I sense in the deer. I assume it is due to the rut season, which has just begun. The bucks are in town.

In rutting season, the bucks are welcomed back by the does from their more isolated region, somewhere outside of this neighborhood. In the spring and summer, the only bucks we see are young ones, yearlings with fuzzy little antlers. But in the fall, they are here in town for a couple months.

This evening several of the deer I know—a couple bucks and yearlings—seem tense, more twitchy than usual. Deer I haven't seen for several weeks are walking into the yard, acknowledging me and then leaving, unsettled. I can feel something is happening, but I can't tell what it is.

"*Snort! Sfoossh!*" I hear from across the street. The sound is loud and unfamiliar. It is coming from Mary. She snorts again, sharply, looking up the alley. Her head is high, the energy is tense, and she is more alert than I've ever seen her. Marta, standing next to her, looks confused, afraid.

Mary turns and bolts around the corner, galloping with all four legs at once. Each landing at least a dozen feet from the first. Marta races to catch up to her, bouncing—no kidding—six feet in the air. She looks more like a circus animal or a gazelle in Africa than a four-month-old fawn.

Turning to look down the alley, I see another doe, a yearling, about four houses down, her ears large and erect, standing in the middle of the alley and looking straight at me. She's unmoving. I hear noises behind me, and Marta jumps out of the bushes with Mary right behind her, so fast that everything is starting to feel like a dream. I'm confused because only minutes ago, they were running in the same direction. Are they racing in a circle around the block? Mary's energy is fierce. She passes me only about six feet away. I can hear her breath, intense and hot. If I were in her way, I would have been trampled.

Feeling some alarm, I turn around to face the yearling down the alley again. And between us, about twenty yards away, walks an adult mountain lion.

The mountain lion is easily 120 pounds, as tall as my hip. Her head and paws look huge, even at this distance. I've never seen a big cat in the wild before, much less in my front yard. The lion moves purposefully but not swiftly, neither looking toward me nor the yearling. She is focused forward, walking from one side of the alley to the other. Where Mary and Marta just ran.

I move purposefully *and* swiftly back to my house to make sure my cat is inside and to freak the hell out. I pace around the house muttering with fear for sweet Marta's life. And yet the awe of the mountain lion's presence is not lost on me. She is a magnificent being, and my flummoxed excitement for the opportunity to see her made my brain stop working. The presence of this wild predator sent fear throughout my body without my permission or will. I read that only two people have been killed in Whatcom County by a mountain lion in the last one hundred years. The chances of this cat choosing me for dinner are very slim, but my body doesn't know that.

Two people die from car accidents every forty hours in Washington, and yet we don't bother coming unglued about getting in our cars every day. But when a wild predator is seen near humans, the intense reaction reveals both our deep disconnection and the memory we've tried to erase of our place in the system as prey.

The deer are made to react to precisely *this* predator. They live on edge, waiting for the inevitability of exactly this situation. It's as if Mary were made for this moment; she has been awakened into a fierceness that I've never witnessed before. She is more ferocious than the mountain lion.

I want to do *something*, but I know there's nothing I can do. I get in the car to drive around the neighborhood to see if I can see either Mary or the lion again. And . . . do what? Place my car in the way between them?

I return home and pray that the mountain lion finds bunnies instead. Suddenly the baby bunnies I thought I cared about but don't really have a relationship with seem more expendable. I note this callous calculation. But I don't know how else to hold the cognitive dissonance racing through my veins. The lion needs to eat too.

The next morning I get up early to look for my friends. I am aware of both an energy of disruption in the air and my own vulnerability, an unfamiliar sensation. Across the street, in the same place where the drama began the previous night, Marta is lying down, resting. And I am relieved to see her mama grazing peacefully nearby. I praise them both for their courage and leadership. It is clear that Mary was circling the lion. She'd transformed from the gentle mama who trusts me to watch over her little one into a fierce matriarch, called into action to protect not just her own fawn but the whole herd.

Mary is limping, which doesn't surprise me. She was animated by some kind of Artemis-like deer goddess last night, with strength beyond her normal capacity. It's like when you hear about those people who can lift a car when their child is pinned under it. It will take her a while to recover. And the mountain lion is not going away. She lives in this neighborhood too. I sense a vulnerability I've never felt before, walking the sidewalks at night, and I wonder at the cost of my previous false sense of security. How it contributed to our perceived disconnection with the rest of the living and dying world.

* * *

I know that wilderness is not all fuzzy fawns sleeping in your garden. Wilderness is also fierce and disinterested. The powerful elements of storm and fire and earthquake cause indiscriminate devastation to all beings in their paths. Sometimes the moment of connection with a wild being that you've been longing to connect with turns into four hours in the ER waiting for five rabies shots. This is what just happened when my sister and her daughter met a friendly but wobbly wild fox who turned out to be rabid. Wilderness is a place where wild animals can tear you apart. And yes, they might. Predation is the way life works.

We humans in the Western world have built walls so thick between us and the rest of the world that we can no longer feel the vulnerability that we actually share with all the others. We try so hard to shield ourselves from our own mortality that we forget that we live in a world that functions through a system of predation. We try to hide from the reality that for any being to stay alive, another being must die.

And it happens every moment. Every time we eat food, we need to take in the life force from another being—a carrot, a chicken, an apple—for us to stay alive. With every breath we inhale, we must take in oxygen that has been released from the bodies of trees and other beings. And we release atoms of our own carbon when we exhale. This carbon isn't just some kind of excess from what we've inhaled; we actually metabolically give up tiny bits of our own carbon-created bodies. Every cell of life must die in order for the whole being to continue to live. Cancer is a cell that refuses to die. It therefore kills the whole system.

We humans don't like it when our mask of protection is pierced. And we react violently. We prefer to imagine that "predator" is our rightful place in the circle of life. We can't tolerate the idea of being prey at all.

How dare a wild animal see *us*, the dominant and privileged human beings, as potential food? When we see a predator in town, our first reaction is to annihilate them. A guy who just moved here from Cordova, Alaska, told me about how the climate crisis has impacted the bears there. In 2018, there was a poor run of pink salmon, and unseasonably long rainy weather also decreased the berry supply. Both berries and salmon are primary food sources for the black bears, whose population is already in steep decline thanks to hunting "harvests." So that fall, the bears were forced to come into the towns where the fishermen were catching silver salmon from the ocean. Fishermen say that they had never seen a bear on the docks in their lifetime. In the fall of 2018, having not caused damage of any kind, thirty-two bears were shot and killed for the crime of standing too close to humans.

Insisting that we should never be vulnerable leads us to do irrational things that break the system. Mountain lions, wolves, and bears have been hunted to near extinction in state-sponsored predator-control programs. The federal government, through the "Wildlife Services" program of the USDA "serves wildlife" by killing more than one hundred thousand carnivores every year. And they are blatant about it. They say they do it to protect the flocks of sheep and cows that are regarded as human property.

The idea of private property is a colonizer privilege woven so deeply into the Western worldview that it is nearly impossible to imagine life in any other way. There is a weird underlying belief that because someone has paid someone who paid someone who paid someone who made up this system, we have the right to treat the land and the creatures there any way we want. Protecting "private property" in America is considered more important than protecting people, animals, water, air, soil, or any of the other foundational threads in the web of life.

My neighbor hates the deer. He expresses outrage when they wander onto "his property," stumbling over himself down his porch steps to chase away any who trespass onto his yard and eat his flowers. "Get out of here, you filthy mangy deer!" he shouts. It's a futile annoyance. They are not going away. This was their territory first.

Deer are adaptive creatures. They find ways to survive even as their habitat of brush and meadow is replaced with lawns and fences. Black-tailed deer are so connected with their territory that they have been known to starve if their food sources are scarce rather than move to another territory beyond their own. They are indigenous, which the dictionary defines as "originating or occurring naturally in a particular place; native." The mountain lions who depend on the deer are usually very reclusive, but they've been forced by human development to move into so-called human territory to survive. In other words, the deer and the mountain lions are indigenous to this place. Not me. Not my cranky neighbor. Not the flowers growing in his yard.

We are the immigrants, the trespassers who moved in and reorganized their habitat. And we act like it's an affront to our privileged sense of ownership that they dare continue to exist. God forbid that deer actually need to do alive things like eat and poop. "Just not *on my* property" is the white privileged refrain.

In an open letter to "America, Colonists, Allies, and Ancestors-yet-to-be," Robin Wall Kimmerer challenges us to make a choice about this very refrain. Addressing the *windigo*, "the name for that which cares more for itself than for anything else," she challenges the colonizer worldview that condemns creatures, places, and elements of the natural world to be treated only as "natural resources," here solely to serve humans. She offers instead the Native worldview on how to relate to the land and all the creatures who live on this planet with us.

> We call them home. We call them our sustainer, our
> library, our pharmacy, our sacred places. Indigenous

identity and language are inseparable from land. Land
is the residence of our more-than-human relatives, the
dust of our ancestors, the holder of seeds, the makers of
rain; our teacher. Land is not capital to which we have
property rights; rather it is the place for which we
have moral responsibility in reciprocity for its gift of
life. Here is the question we must at last confront: Is
land merely a source of belongings, or is it the source of
our most profound sense of belonging? We can choose.

We can choose to live within the system of sacred
reciprocity, a more spiritually and physically vital way of
framing the system of predation. We are called throughout
our lives to give of ourselves sacrificially because that's what
love requires. It's also just the way life works.

Remembering the sacrificial nature of life is embedded in the spiritual practice of communion. As Jesus said,
"Greater love has no one than this: to lay down one's life
for one's friends." Wild spirituality invites us to expand
the context of communion to include the wider sense of
sacrifice that keeps the whole cosmic community alive.
My friend, ecotheologian Lisa Dahill, published a radical
article right at the beginning of the COVID-19 pandemic,
calling us to celebrate what she calls our "interspecies vulnerability." She is brilliant in finding ways to integrate the
sacramental practices of the church with the biological
realities of life on this astonishing planet.

Dahill asks readers to imagine what it would take to
"invite us all out of our massive collective cosmological
delusion and denial" of the uncomfortable fact that most

humans prefer to think of ourselves solely as "eaters," yet we are still part of Earth's food web. What would it look like not merely to acknowledge but to celebrate that we are mortal members of a world that remains alive only by consuming one another's lives? Rituals like the sharing of bread and wine to celebrate our communion with the sacred and one another need to be expanded to invite us into our kindred communion with all of life. A communion practice rooted in this biological reality of sacred reciprocity, Dahill says, could be "our re-entry to a world alive with gratitude and grace, wild energy and relationships, calling us to re-join it. Let's come home. With all who eat, as those who are eaten, let us learn to pray."

At Church of the Wild communion rituals, sharing bread and wine—or wild blackberries growing on the edge of our circle and cedar tea we brew during the wanderings—reminds us of our belonging to a larger story. By sharing this symbol of a "meal" together, we remember that we are not only consuming the metaphor of Jesus's body to become the metaphor of Jesus's body on Earth today but also acknowledging that our actual bodies are kept alive by the sacrifice of other bodies, with grapes and wheat as stand-ins for all those we consume. And we are acknowledging that we are here not just to consume but also to be consumed, to offer our lives for others.

* * *

I am not suggesting that we just accept that children playing outside might get eaten by a mountain lion so we shouldn't do anything to protect them. Part of aliveness is a commitment to staying alive. But when *our* own lives are the only lives that matter, we mess with the rules of reality. Love is only present when we love self and at the same time we love the creative world, the neighbor. Love is an equilibrium between your own interests and those of others. When we step out of love, we remove ourselves from the conversation, and we are no longer participating in the presence of Christ. Our mentality of privileged status—meeting our own needs without considering the needs of the others—removes us from the circle of life, which eventually kills the whole system.

What I am suggesting is that we come out of our castles of privilege and rejoin reality. Reality is a system of reciprocity—give and take, not just take—that makes it possible for the life of the whole to continue to thrive and evolve. Remembering that we are connected to a larger story, even if we don't totally understand it, is a radical act of trust and surrender.

Belden Lane talks about how fierce, indifferent landscapes invite us into the sacred. "The divine indifference" in fierce landscapes, he says, is an invitation to relinquish self, to focus on the reality that we are not *experiencing* nature because we *are* nature. "I really don't want a God who is solicitous of my every need, fawning for my attention, eager for nothing in the world so much as the fulfillment of myself-potential." He calls this a "house-broken" God.

I, too, am tired of the tame God and boxed-in Christ, distorted by patriarchy and control-seeking humans who use religion to maintain the status quo. I'm yearning for a wild God that compels me to full participation in this miraculous dance of life, deepening the meaning in a core Jesus saying, "Whoever wants to save their life will lose it, but whoever loses their life for me will find it."

Light is not possible without darkness. Love is not possible without grief and loss. Life is not possible without death. I know this with my head. I don't *like* how death is built into the system. Sometimes it makes me question the whole idea of a compassionate God. But I'm discovering a deep acceptance of death as not just "oh well, it's part of life" but a necessary and even beautiful part of life. I want to feel what Walt Whitman said, "All goes onward and outward, nothing collapses, / And to die is different from what any one supposed, and luckier."

Even though the life-death-new-life story of Jesus was essentially the theme of every single sermon I'd ever delivered, it took an intentional reconnection with the natural world (as it *is*, not as I wish it were) for me to really get it. Sometimes when religious language is repeated enough, you think you understand what you're talking about. "Christ has died. Christ has risen. Christ will come again. Hallelujah." Like when you say any word too many times—"fork fork fork fork"—the words start to warp and lose their meaning, becoming only a collection of sounds. My son tells me it's called "semantic satiation." Sometimes I can hear sacred truths better if they aren't couched in strictly religious language. Then those words give me light to open up the religious language on a deeper level. It's a rhythm that I've come to trust. When words stop making sense to me, I know it is an invitation to dig beneath the emptiness to find new ways to see.

It was Andreas Weber, a German biologist and philosopher, who helped me to see that for a great spiritual truth to be true, it needs to be seen echoing through the physical, creative world. I learned from him that the beautiful forest scene outside my window is beautiful not in *spite* of the reality that half of it is dead or dying but *because* of it. He shows, in accessible biological and poetic language, that love really is at the center of all things.

Weber's glorious chapter on death reads like quantum poetry—if that were a thing—in the vein of Ranier Maria Rilke and Rachel Carson, using the erotic language of Song of Solomon. Weber explains in *Matter and Desire: An Erotic Ecology*, "Just as cells can only survive by casting off their substance and building themselves anew in every moment . . . by cultivating death in all of their actions—we too will only be enlivened when, in the face of the terrors that this life holds in store, we discard our illusions, break open the emotional armor that supposedly protects us against fear but in truth simply causes our souls to harden into prisons."

Facing the legitimately terrifying reality of death is not easy. But denying it and hiding behind illusions of control and prisons of self-protection only serve to disconnect us even more from full participation in the great conversation. To repair the damage we've done to our relationship with Earth, we are invited to allow our hearts to break for the loss and to be opened up to love again. We are invited back into the love story.

We are invited to become like giant sequoia trees, who can only fully reproduce with the assistance of wildfires that destroy the forest but offer their seeds the opportunity to grow. Embracing the mystery of life into death into new life, and offering our own lives to others in sacrificial love, is not just the moral, religious thing to do. It is the way the whole system of life evolves and grows.

*   *   *

Last summer we held a Seminary of the Wild intensive at Ghost Ranch in New Mexico. Ghost Ranch is a retreat center in the high desert, about an hour northwest of Santa Fe. The Pueblo and other First Nations people who first tended this region have a traumatic history there, of wars and colonization and Christianization. But the land speaks of ancient veneration. You can tell it is a sacred place.

Between long wanderings on the land, we offer invitations to connect with your wild self on this wild earth and consider how that changes your sense of the wild Christ. We invited Michael Dowd, a United Church of Christ minister and author of *Thank God for Evolution*, to speak to the implications of the climate crisis on our spiritual journeys. He is an itinerant preacher now, traveling the country with his wife preaching the gospel of what he calls "post-doom spirituality."

Armed with a battery of evidence, graphs, multimedia, data, handouts, and science, Dowd laid out the reality of the global crisis resulting from a species that treats Earth not as kin but as resource. It was overwhelming. Fifteen years ago, we in the climate movement were focused on "ending the climate crisis" so the carbon in the atmosphere wouldn't get above 350 parts per million (ppm). "Game over," we called it, if it did. By 2019, when Dowd was presenting to us, the CO_2 level had already risen above 415 ppm. He showed us how we are losing 428 billion metric tons of ice per year and how, over the last two hundred years, we've destroyed nearly five billion acres of forests. And he shared what has been said so often we almost can't hear it anymore: the current rate of species extinction is higher than any time in history since the collision of space rocks that killed off dinosaurs and most other species on the planet. Only this time we humans are the space rock.

Most of us sitting there were visibly discomfited by the overwhelming tragedies Dowd exposed. I heard things like, "I feel hopeless, why even bother?" and "What's the point of worrying about reducing my consumption if it doesn't make a difference?" and "You can't go overwhelming people like this because they will give up the fight!"

As I sat with my own discomfort, some clarity arose within me. When you get a cancer diagnosis from the doctor, do you say, "Oh, hand me another cigarette and beer; I'll just eat, drink, and be merry these last days"? No, you finally start that exercise routine you've been meaning to start, and you dig into the healthy, organic foods you've been lazy about in your days of mistaken immortality. When your mother's Alzheimer's has gotten so bad that it is clear she will never again be the way you knew her, do you say, "What's the point? She doesn't know me anyway"? You know you're looking at up to ten years of slow, painful, and expensive decline, but do you throw her out onto the streets and console yourself with all the money you've saved? No, you deplete her savings—and your own if you have to—and you exhaust yourself caring for her. Why? Because you love her. Because you love your own life. Because life is worth it.

Our initial reactions of resistance to the reality of the mortal wounds we've inflicted on Mother Earth reveals a lack of connection, a gap where love should be. This is how I understand Michael Dowd's post-doom spirituality. This is a spirituality that accepts the fullness of our reality: the tragedy as well as the beauty. This spirituality moves into—and then eventually beyond—grief and repentance toward a deeper, more courageous, compassionate, and spiritual aliveness. Post-doom spirituality is, Dowd says, "what opens up when we remember who we are, accept the inevitable, honor our grief, and prioritize what is pro-future and soul-nourishing. A fierce and fearless reverence for life."

Dowd credits his cancer diagnosis, years earlier, for his shift in perspective. He knew he could no longer put off the deep, relational work he needed to do with those closest to him. Facing your own mortality without a place to hide boils things down to the essentials and helps you release fantasy and projections. What remains, he says, is relationship. Dowd calls himself a "reality mystic" who accepts that nothing is permanent. Honoring what is real and grieving what must end grounds you in gratitude, and you become free to commit to being a blessing to those you love.

Facing the reality that we're standing on a precipice right now, as a species and as a whole planet, is sobering, to say the least. But facing what is real opens the heart to grief, which somehow opens the heart to love even more deeply. Denial requires that we shut ourselves off, build walls around our hearts out of self-protection. But that self-protection can become a prison, as Andreas Weber says. We can't shut off *parts* of our hearts. Trying to not feel the pain of the world also cuts us off from the pain of our children when they need us most, and from the children of other mothers who are suffering.

Love requires that we feel the pain of our beloveds. Only by facing the reality of their suffering can we grieve. Only when we grieve can we love again. Reckoning with grief at that level is difficult because you're afraid you might die. And that's the point. Grief brings screams of pain that cause you to wrap your knees up to your stomach and try to breathe between the sobs for the loss of all that is worth loving.

And *after* that? When you're exhausted and have expressed all you can express and your body has nothing more to say, then there is a deep calm. This emptiness is necessary to make room for a deeper spiritual connection, free from both denial and despair.

Gerald May, psychiatrist, theologian, spiritual director, and author, wrote his last book, *The Wisdom of Wilderness*, when he was fifty years old. As he was battling cancer, he felt compelled to immerse himself in the wilderness. He describes how nature "acquainted me with my own inner nature: how external wilderness spoke to my internal wilderness, and how it healed me and made me more whole." He died only months later.

Describing a night of camping alone in a small tent, May writes that he awoke to a bear brushing up against his tent with a deep, slow growl. Being that close to the raw power of a giant predator caused pure, naked terror that froze his body and awakened all of his senses. God, in the form of a feminine presence he calls the "Power of the Slowing," whispered to him about what he needed to do, "Be frightened. Just be frightened." He did what he was told, and the paradox happened to him, "My heart is beating so loudly I'm sure the bear must hear it. And I have never felt so alive."

When you reconnect with the alive world in a more compassionate way, and when you realize that the whole world is a living system that can only thrive when death makes room for new life, you may feel a calm settle into you. You may find yourself with the energy that comes from love to embrace the whole story, including the necessary emptiness and loss.

"It is not enough to weep for our lost landscapes; we have to put our hands in the earth to make ourselves whole again," writes Robin Wall Kimmerer. "Even a wounded world is feeding us. Even a wounded world holds us, giving us moments of wonder and joy. I choose joy over despair." Post-doom spirituality ultimately chooses joy over despair. It is a shift away from our capitalistic productivity goals that aim to "fix global warming" (as if the not-so-bad-sounding "warming" were simply something broken that needs a man to fix it). This is a wild spirituality that loves the world for the sake of the good of the world itself. For the sake of the trees still living and the waters still flowing and the doe you've grown to love who is protecting her herd. And the mountain lion who may take the doe's baby to feed her own.

This is a spirituality beyond the "cure" mentality: the mentality that marginalizes people with disabilities such as blindness or muscular dystrophy as victims in constant need of being fixed. While medical research to treat such disabilities remains important, many people with incurable conditions long for support, like all of us do, to live their highest quality of life. Appreciated and valued just as they are.

When we look toward what has been lost with the climate crisis or other ecological damage that our species has inflicted, we do still need to strive toward repair, but the cure is within our own mentality. The mentality that love really is as strong as death (like the beloved says to the lover in Song of Solomon) compels us to regard those of us who remain—forests, polar bears, wilderness, people—with fierce love, looking toward how we can all live our highest quality of life together as beloved community, no matter what.

We do not need to minimize or overlook the pain and tragedy we encounter as we live in this time of interwoven crises. Eventually, when we recognize that the pain is directly connected with our love, we can embrace it. We can move into actions of restoration that are firmly planted in love.

* * *

My beloved Mary and her sweet fawn Marta have not returned since the mountain lion drama. It's been weeks. I miss them with an ache in my chest and a pit in my stomach. I try convincing myself that they're all right, which allows me to keep focused on my work. I can only assume that the appearance of the predator signaled an end to this neighborhood as a safe territory. It sounds trite, but I've been saying this a lot lately: "It is what it is." She may show up tomorrow or she may never return. I cannot control her, nor do I want to. I just continue to love her.

These deer friends, these kin, are an echo of the sacred to me. Even their absence speaks of the presence of an invisible web of holiness connecting me with them, and through them to a deeper connection with life. Christ as Conversation includes the conversation between predator and prey. It may not be a particularly nice conversation, especially if you're the prey. But it is a real one. And I am not interested in anything less.

A life lived in love requires an open and broken heart, exposed and willing to show up every day. Every small sadness and every small joy might bring tears and sometimes sobs that you can't control. Maybe it's backed up.

The cougar's presence released these tears in me. The fragile dam I've erected out of self-protection cracked with a deep fissure. So many years of holding it together. Every day this week, I've felt myself on the edge, holding back the glacial waters with this roughly hewn dam that takes all my fingers and toes to plug the holes. And it's not just the mountain lion; all of life right now feels like we are living an epic myth, like we are standing on our front porch and watching a jet headed for our house in slow motion, and we can't move. We can only stare as it heads toward our own demise.

Last night, as I was sitting on the porch, for a minute (or was it ten?) I didn't hear anything but human hums: the leaf blower, the car, the train, the dog bark. Something irrational in me panicked; was this the silence Rachel Carson warned would happen some spring? Is her *Silent Spring* fully here today? Because we all live on the edge now. New changes, new tragedies happen so often these days that we expect almost anything. What else is ending? The sun could come up tomorrow blood red and we would say "Yes, this is the new way. Okay."

In the midst of the many layers of the unknown we face at this moment in history, I turn to a mystic whose brilliant life was interrupted by cruelty beyond imagination. Dutch author Etty Hillesum articulated the deepest contours of a post-doom and wild spirituality better than anyone I've ever heard. I first read her remarkable diary, *An Interrupted Life*, when I was in college, before I even knew I was searching for a spiritual life.

Hillesum was Jewish, and in 1942 she could have escaped the atrocities of the Holocaust, but she refused to do so. She stayed with her friends and family and was murdered with them in Auschwitz, having claimed that to go into hiding "would bring a different kind of death, a death that is a postponement of living." She wrote,

I have looked our destruction, our miserable end . . . straight in the eye and accepted it into my life, and my love of life has not been diminished. . . .

. . . The misery here is quite terrible; and yet, late at night when the day has slunk away into the depths behind me, I often walk with a spring in my step along the barbed wire. And then time and again, it soars straight from my heart—I can't help it, that's just the way it is, like some elementary force—the feeling that life is glorious and magnificent, and that one day we shall be building a whole new world.

9
Wild Ordination

Go out in the woods, go out.
If you don't go out in the woods nothing will ever happen
and your life will never begin.

—Clarissa Pinkola Estés, *Women*
Who Run with the Wolves
20th century CE

I sense that Etty Hillesum's feeling that "one day we shall be building a whole new world" is happening. The new story that Thomas Berry called for nearly fifty years ago is emerging, even as the old story is kicking and screaming in resistance. Berry's intention for his work was to evoke the "psychic and spiritual resources to establish a new reciprocity of humans with Earth and of humans to one another." Wild church is a way to put those resources into practice in service of the inner and outer transformation desperately needed at this moment in history. Berry is confident that "with a change of worldview will come an appropriately comprehensive ethics of reverence for all life. With a new perspective regarding our place in this extraordinary unfolding of Earth history will emerge a renewed awareness of our role in guiding the evolutionary process at this crucial point in history."

As we respond to the call of nature inviting us into the sacred, we can become vessels of healing and restoration. The new story won't be written by experts negotiating terms at the UN or a new set of progressive politicians coming into power or any kind of top-down plan. This new world-view will come into being through *us*. Berry's vision, the new story, is unfolding as you and I and millions of others say yes to the call from Earth and Spirit to escort this new, compassionate story of reverent reciprocity into the world.

Discerning our particular roles requires that we recognize and step into our greatest gifts, often constructed from the ashes of our deepest wounds. The call comes from within kindred relationship, as we commit ourselves to what Bill Plotkin says is "the largest story we're capable of living, serving something bigger than ourselves. We must dare again to dream the impossible and to romance the world, to feel and honor our kinship with all species and habitats, to embrace the troubling wisdom of paradox, and to shape ourselves into visionaries with the artistry to revitalize our enchanted and endangered world."

Parker J. Palmer, in his inspiring book on vocation, says that calling, at its deepest level, is "something I can't not do, for reasons I'm unable to explain to anyone else and don't fully understand myself but that are nonetheless compelling." Calling requires a reckoning with who you are in your most wild essence, paying attention to your unique vulnerabilities. What breaks your heart and makes you cry? There's a clue. Authentic callings are usually unexpected and also somehow deeply familiar. At first you may be shocked by the glimpses of who you actually are capable of being. Eventually, though, the call settles in and you are like, "Ah, yes, I have been preparing for this all my life."

* * *

All morning this raven had been taunting me. Have you heard the mocking laugh of ravens? I'm more familiar with the *caw* of crows, so the more intense *kraak* of the raven is an alluring curiosity I could not resist. I was sure this raven was determined to wake me up before the others gathered for breakfast. When I unzipped my tent, I saw a doe looking at me from across the small meadow, as if waiting for me.

It was the first day of a five-day wilderness soul program, guided by Geneen Marie Haugen. Twenty of us gathered to explore what it means to be "Coming Home to an Animate World," the title of the intensive, to "engage in conversations with sacred Others—whom we might know as stone, river, owl or pinyon, or as a figure from a dream, or as soul, anima, beloved or muse, or simply as world."

The conversation began immediately, on the first morning, with this raven. I threw my shoes on quickly and decided to try and follow the raven's call even though birds are a little difficult to chase. The doe had vanished, as they can so easily. As I jumped over her matted-down nest, I wondered if she had stationed herself in front of my tent on purpose. Dismissing the thought, I trailed along the rocky deer path in a rather lame attempt to catch up to the squawking trickster. This, before coffee.

With the raven still in sight ahead of me, a massive bird approached from behind, flying over my head. She was close enough to feel her presence, though her flight was silent. The wingspan was at least four feet wide, maybe five. I didn't catch her face; I just knew I've never seen a bird this large, certainly not this close. I slowed down, stunned, accepting that I could never catch up with them.

Later in the week, returning to camp from wandering along the river in the early afternoon, I heard the raven again. Flying directly in front of me, across the trail, she headed into the wooded forest to my right. Without thinking, I pivoted and followed her easily enough to watch her land on a branch not far from the ground, maybe fifteen feet up. On the branch below sat a magnificent, regal great horned owl.

The majesty of this encounter! I had no thoughts. No words from Spirit or owl. Just a deep, quiet gratitude for the gift of her royal presence. It was only about three in the afternoon, early for a reclusive owl to be awake and voluntarily visible by the likes of me. I sat down slowly and leaned back to admire her for nearly a half hour. I was late to return to the group, but I didn't care; I wasn't going to leave until she dismissed me.

She looked around slowly, regarding her kingdom. The raven left after a few minutes, her role complete. The owl gazed periodically down at me, her eyes holding mine, her lids closing slowly in an intentional blink. The minutes seemed like non-time. I wished I had my camera, but I also knew she would not have given me the permission. Royalty can be like that. The pure gift of her attention shot a peace through my flesh as deep as the deepest meditative state I'd ever achieved.

After about a half hour, she turned her body completely around, lifted her layers of speckled tail feathers, and pooped. Then she flew away, officially ending my appointment with her. I grabbed my backpack to rush back to the human circle to tell the others of my remarkable encounter.

Before I made it back to the trail, though, a still small voice from deep within me said, without adornment, "You need to be ordained by the wild."

In that moment, I did what one must do in the presence of the holy: I fell to my knees and sobbed until the tears were spent. I didn't even really know what it meant, but I knew from where the voice had come. It was the voice of the Christ, and the voice of the owl, and the voice of my soul, all three in one. I am not ordained by an institution or a denomination. I'd worked in independent churches where ordination isn't a big deal my whole pastoral career, and I'd always felt a little insecure about it.

I walked another six feet and the voice said, "You need to be baptized by the wild." I stood there without words and lowered my head, unable to move, as if in prayer. But it was a different way of prayer that needs no amen at the end because I am the amen. "May it be so," I said quietly anyway. And after another three steps, I heard one more implausible and ridiculous summons: "Rewild the church."

* * *

What does it mean to be ordained by the wild? How am *I* supposed to rewild the church? When you find yourself on the receiving end of an implausible and ridiculous call, it is a good idea to hold it closely, reverently, and with tender curiosity. And don't waste too much time trying to figure it out. The call comes from Mystery, which remains mysterious no matter what.

Saying yes to an implausible calling into full participation with the Great Story actually requires a kind of arrogance. An "arrogance of belonging" is what David Whyte named it when talking about what we need in order to live our most creative and adventurous and expressive lives. Considering Whyte's idea, Elizabeth Gilbert wrote that the arrogance of belonging is not about self-absorption or self-judgment (which are forms of arrogance) but "a force that will actually take you [out of yourself] and allow you to engage more fully with the world." The arrogance of belonging simply says, "I am here. I belong here. I have a role here in the whole." It took me a while to learn that.

At this threshold of collapse and new life where we are standing now, our full engagement is too urgently needed to mess around with false humility. It takes a degree of arrogance, holy arrogance of belonging, to say yes and step into the unknown, trusting that you will know what to do as you take the steps. Holy arrogance is also paradoxically humble. As part of a great, interconnected story, we are never called to act alone.

I have no illusions that I am single-handedly responsible for "rewilding the church." The sacred experience with a great horned owl does, though, helped me discern the seeds of purpose in my life. I remain an edge walker on the fringe of the Christ tradition, even as I reckon with the multiple extreme and heartbreaking ways the church has harmed people. Still, I love her in her brokenness and cannot fully walk away. I did for seven years, and I needed to. But now I feel compassion for the wild truth and love embodied by Jesus, which has been buried beneath centuries of distortion by men who didn't get it. And I feel wholehearted about the vocation of reconnecting nature and spirit, church and wild.

The roles you will be asked to step into will require the full expression of your own unique gifts and will ask you to offer them "to assist the world in renewing herself," as storyteller and truth sayer Michael Meade puts it. He uses the term *genius* to describe the unique gifts and essence of each person, called into service to the world: "As resident spirit of the soul, the genius in each of us is both our natural connection to nature and our secret connection to the divine." Intimacy with nature, he agrees, helps us to remember that we belong to a greater story. Our call is to learn our unique and important role in advancing that story. Meade asks, "Could nature, now overburdened and sorely mistreated, be calling on each of us to take up the thread of genius that is closest to our own nature and set to the work of helping to reimagine and reweave the whole divine thing?" I think so.

Ordain means "to command, to destine, to order." To be ordained is to be called into service, to accept holy orders. It is a sacrament in the Christian tradition and also practiced in Buddhism, Judaism, and, with different words, in just about every other tradition as well. Ordination is not necessarily just for priests either. An ordination is important to ritually mark a vow of fidelity to a calling.

At first, ordination just meant an order for a particular vocation. From the queens to the priests to the ones who lit the candles, all were ordained with respectful ceremonies. But in the twelfth century, something happened with Christian ordination. Given the problems the church was creating as it distorted itself with state power, it is not surprising that ordination shifted. It became a ritual that affirmed only religious vocation, which appropriated power to men (and only men), elevating them above the "laity." Women who were already ordained—and there were many women leaders in the church until then—were actually *un*ordained. It took another eight centuries to undo their undoing.

Without getting too caught up in the stupidness of powerful men in charge of the church in the Middle Ages and beyond, I do want to honor the sacrament of ordination and imagine what a wild ordination might look like. How could ordination help us to treat the vows we have made or will make to serve the world—the whole, wild world—with dignity?

I am not suggesting an institutional ritual. Wild ordination is not even an essential part of starting a wild church community (though you may want to consider it if you *do* start your own church of the wild). But I looked into the diverse ordination processes for several different denominations and found that there are some commonalities. Most of them included these steps: a call, a preparation, lots of committees and questions to answer, a ceremony, and placement into service.

* * *

In wild ordination, it is the wild that calls you into service. It's not the hierarchy. The calling comes when it comes, from whomever it comes, and at the right time. I can't be more specific than that. Because I don't know. Only you will know. What I do know is that we are deeply interconnected with a world yearning to be whole again. I have heard people say that Earth doesn't need humans for her wholeness, and that without humans, Earth would be just fine thank you. I get it. But we are part of Earth and our stubborn attempts to disconnect have led to an unraveling that affects not just the parts (species extinction, habitat destruction, wars, and oppression) but the whole. There must be an essential role that humans play in the whole system's healing as well.

Even the Bible—used often throughout history to dislocate people from the web of interbeing—is actually quite eloquent about the reality of a cosmos that yearns for our full participation and mutual healing. Most dramatically, there's this important passage that I've cited many times over the past quarter century as evidence of a suffering and compassionate planet, the one about "the whole creation, groaning as if in childbirth." I felt drawn to dig more deeply into the meaning of this text when I was referring to it during a course at Seminary of the Wild. I translated it myself from the Greek text to dig past my too-familiar ways of reciting it and to scrape aside patriarchal interpretations that may have influenced my understanding. Here is my rendering of Romans 8:15–23, from Paul's most impassioned letter that reveals a solid cosmology of our deep interconnection with the whole earth:

> For you did not receive a spirit of slavery that returns you to fear, but you received the Spirit of Kinship, with whom we cry, "Abba! Father! Mama! Mother!" Spirit bears witness with our own wild souls, reminding us that we are coinhabitants, living in utter interdependence with All. And as kin we inherit our place in the land, participants in Christ, if indeed we feel the pain together, so that we, with all beings, may be celebrated together.
>
> Consider that the sufferings of our present times are not as weighty as the lingering presence of the Sacred that will be fully revealed in us all.
>
> The whole creation longs with eager expectation for this unveiling of the human, beloved ones. For Earth was subjected to emptiness not of her own choice, but out of a pattern of life and death, in hope that the creation,

herself, will be set free from her own spirit of slavery to decay and brought into glorious freedom, alongside the freedom of their human kin.

We know that the whole creation has been groaning together, in the pains of childbirth, until this present time. Not only them, as if they were separate, but we ourselves, who have been awakened by Mystery, we, too, groan inwardly as we eagerly await our reconnection as kin within the whole, a full release from our collective bondage to a culture of destruction into a fully restored and embodied web of life.

The biologist Andreas Weber relates the same message for us today: "Earth is currently suffering from a shortage of our love." Falling in love with particular places and beings, like particular people, means that we open our hearts to groan as we feel the pain of the others as our own. The whole creation is waiting for the awakening of wild human souls to restore the broken relationship, in all the magnificently diverse ways. We are all in this together.

Buddhist mystic and spiritual ecologist Joanna Macy told a story during a recent webinar with Seminary of the Wild that she has told many times before. She recounted a meeting with deep ecologist John Seed, who is a radically successful forest activist. When Joanna asked him how he had the courage to stand there, alone, facing giant bull-dozers meant to destroy an ancient forest, he said that he sensed the forest rising behind him. He felt himself rooted in the immensely larger beings that had called him into service. He said, "I was no longer John Seed, protecting the rainforest. I was the rainforest protecting herself through this little piece of humanity I cradled into existence."

It is worth saying again: we are not separate from nature. We simply are a part of nature that comes in this particular human form, with our own particular interests and gifts and flaws and voice. We humans who can hear the call are urgently needed. The rainforest is calling us, the deer are calling us, the open vast sky suffering invisibly with too much carbon is calling us, the rabid fox is calling us. What is your role in this love story of reconnection, restoration, and compassion? What part of the sacred wild is calling you to be ordained into service on her behalf?

* * *

Many religious ordinations require an extended time of preparation: seminary, internships, spiritual direction, and so on. I think the word that fits a wild ordination would be something like *apprenticeship*. When you hear a call from the wild, it can take years to live into it. Apprenticing to those beings or places that reveal the sacred to you is an act of learning from them, honoring their wisdom, and learning skills.

My son first heard a call from Earth when he was twelve and began speaking out against the climate crisis. At thirteen, he created SLAP, the Sea Level Awareness Project, an installation of ten-foot poles along the beach that warned of the dangers of sea-level rise. Now, thirteen years later, he has taken that ordination vow deeper. He has apprenticed himself to the wild edge of a particular shoreline in Washington.

After several years of depression following his activism burnout, Alec found refuge and healing at the edge of the southern Salish Sea within sight of the state capitol building in Olympia. There is a particular place where a small creek flows to the bay through a concrete pipe, and here he has returned again and again, answering the call into relationship.

Over the last three years, he has spent more than five hundred hours with this shore, taking nearly half a million photos and hundreds of hours of video. His journals are thousands of pages long, capturing intimate encounters with many species in the bay. He has met particular ducks, geese, crows, gulls, hummingbirds and songbirds, bald eagles and hawks, seals and river otters, trees and small plants, shells and driftwood, and countless stones, barnacles, crabs, and seaweeds. He tracks sunrises and sunsets, winters and summers, high tides and low tides. Watching as the creek floods and the land erodes into the sea, plants grow and die, animals return again, he has fallen in love. This shore, and all who live there, are his teachers.

Alec, in intimate relationship with this place, has activated a call to turn this deep, attentive romance into a multimedia expression that invites others into the sacred presence of this shoreline. By connecting with city officials, local Indigenous tribes, and other stakeholders, he will work to rewild this place and restore a sense of communal belonging. His project also invites others to fall in love with their own home places by providing a platform for sharing these stories. Ordained by the wild, he is committed to restoring our relationship with our places by re-storying them.

* * *

In institutional ordinations in the Catholic and most other mainstream Christian traditions, the bishops personally anoint the next generations as priests so there is an "apostolic succession." This means your ordination is the latest in a legacy of ordained priests that is connected all the way back to the apostle Peter, who was commissioned by Jesus.

In wild ordination, the succession of relationships began with the first explosive bang of energy some thirteen billion years ago ("in the beginning was the Conversation") and you, living right now, are the latest being, a human, drawn into the holy orders of a wild, glorious world.

A friend of mine, Veronica Kyle, shared the story of discovering her wild calling during a webinar she led at Seminary of the Wild. She began, "Nature was unsafe for those who look like me." Veronica is part of the diaspora of Black families who left the South and migrated North. Until she was eight, she and her family lived in Anniston, Alabama, a place infamous for the Ku Klux Klan's burning of the Freedom Riders' bus in 1961 and subsequent beating of the passengers as they fled the fire. Anniston is also where many of her relatives died from Monsanto's poisoning of their watershed. Her family moved from one community burdened by toxic chemicals to a concrete

housing project on the far south side of Chicago, surrounded again by industry, known as the "toxic doughnut."

Moving to the city from the country also meant losing a
loving relationship she had built with nature. In particular,
she spoke affectionately about her relationship with the
trees, climbing them and playing under them in her early
years. In the urban North, connecting with nature meant
you were a "country bumpkin," and the nearby woods
were to be avoided. Due to the horrific racist encounters
that Black families had experienced, nature was considered
dangerous, dirty, and forbidden.

As a young child, Veronica was told, "We're moving
North so you can get a good education. Then you can use
your head, not your hands to make a living." This statement
alone sent a message to her that getting one's hands dirty
"was not what Black folks needed to be doing."

In college, Veronica immersed herself in the lineage
of Black women theologians whose connection with
the sacred is intimately joined with the natural world:
Katie Cannon, Delores Williams, Anna Julia Cooper, Emi-
lie Townes, Rev. Anita Bryant, Stephanie Y. Evans, and
Marsha Harris, to name a few. She calls these women her
spiritual ancestors on whose shoulders she stands. I might
call them members of her human apostolic lineage. As she
found her voice and a place to stand among her elders,
she also found her way back to the trees and to a broader
spirituality that integrated her religious heritage and her
deep connection with the natural world.

She felt called, ordained by the wild. Veronica reclaimed
her ancestral connection with herbs and midwifery and

divine womanist wisdom. She made a commitment to embody her call fully as an *ecowomanist*, one whose environmental activism is centered in "the voices of women of African descent and women of color." She and her covisionary, Valerie Rawls, recently launched the EcoWomanist Institute as a reconnector to the natural world for her Black and Brown sisters.

* * *

In an institutional ordination, you often have to study to come up with the right answers to the questions you're asked by a thousand committees. But in a wild ordination, the questions come more in the form of a conversation, and there are never wrong answers. The committees are diverse interactions with trees and gnats and sunsets, and they meet at unexpected moments like when the crimson leaves let go and fall to the ground or the shoreline erodes suddenly into the sea. The conversation weaves a new story within you. And you, in turn, help to weave the new story emerging through all of us.

Ordination ceremonies in churches are usually a big deal: a full mass with regalia and choirs and bishops, and there's usually a confirmation question or twenty asked. Something like, "And will you, in accordance with the canons of this Church, obey your bishop and other ministers who may have authority over you and your work?" Obedience is unsurprisingly important in an institutional ordination.

In a wild ordination, the questions you might be asked are more along the lines of the first ordination, issued by

Jesus to Peter at the shore, beside his boat where he was fishing. Using the language of deep relationality, Jesus asked him, "Peter, do you love me?" And Peter said something like, "Oh my God, yes, I love you." Three times Peter affirmed his love. Three times Jesus said to him, "Okay, then, go feed my sheep."

"Do you love me?" Earth asks, the deer ask, the remaining oak tree in the park asks. And you say yes.

"Will you speak for those whose voices have not been heard?" And you say yes.

"Will you represent the wild ones whose authentic worth has been disregarded for too many generations, to recover and rescue and restore them?" And you say yes in the way only you can. "Okay, well done, go and feed my sheep." And so you do. In the way only you can.

* * *

Unlike many institutional ordination processes that require a placement in a church before you can be called "reverend," the particular form of a wildly ordained calling is not rigidly defined. Different forms will likely offer themselves to you throughout your life. The calling is about you being fully you in service to the rest of the world as you are uniquely needed. This sounds vague, I know. It has something to do with allowing yourself to love what you love. All you can do is say yes to the invitation and allow that sacred *yes* to flow through you as if by a holy wind, whipping around the rocks and trees and through you and back again into the world.

Your own wildly ordained service could take any number of forms. The implausible calls from the sacred heard through relationship with great horned owls or a colony of bees or a field of marigolds or even a glimmer in your child's eye are never meant to be realized fully on your own.

It's like the old story about the three sisters who responded to the problem of the babies drowning in the river. It's told in many different ways. I tell it this way: One sister ran to rescue as many babies as she could, urging her two sisters to come join her. But her two sisters run away, up the river. The second sister went to see where the children were falling in and began building fences and barriers to protect them. She called to her sister, "Help me! There is too much work to do this on my own!" But the third sister ran farther up the river to the village to teach the children how to swim. Joanna Macy tells this story through the three dimensions of the Great Turning: (1) actions to slow the damage to Earth and its beings, (2) analysis of structural causes and the creation of structural alternatives, and (3) shift in consciousness. The moral of this story is summarized in Mark Pullam, elder of the Confederated Tribes of Siletz, in the question he asks at the end: "Which sister did the right thing?"

The answer, of course, is that *all* the sisters did the right thing. They saved the babies not because of any one of their efforts but because of all of them. All of our efforts are important, and we need one another—or our implausible callings do become impossible.

The work we are all being called to do to restore relationship with the earth as sacred is both dangerous and liberating. The system won't like it. Living true to your wild ordination and reconnecting with the wild sacred disrupts the status quo. It is inherently countercultural because we are creating a new, more compassionate, and regenerative culture and community and religion and everything. You might get called a pantheist or a heretic or a dirt-worshipping tree hugger. You might get accused of leading the sheep astray. But we are simply leading the sheep back into the wilderness where they belong.

This new story will come into being through what systems thinker and writer Margaret Wheatley calls *emergence*. In her article outlining stages of emergence, she explains, "Emergence violates so many of our Western assumptions of how change happens. . . . In nature, change never happens as a result of top-down, preconceived strategic plans. . . . Change begins as local actions spring up simultaneously in many different areas. . . . When they become connected, local actions can emerge as a powerful system with influence at a more global or comprehensive level." By connecting our small, local actions, we are making the pathway together.

We are making the road by walking, as poet Antonio Machado says. Nobody has all the answers. There are no operating manuals. This kin-dom of God, the new and yet ancient story, is emerging through *us*. We are defining what the world will be like for our great-grandchildren and for the remaining species on Earth. We are forging new ways, like deer paths, off the trail. For those who are rushing by, the deer paths are overlooked, nearly invisible. But if you are wandering slowly, pausing to listen for the sacred sparkling in the raindrops on the tips of the needles in the trees, you'll see the trails easily.

My deer friends, Mary and Marta, did return a few weeks after the mountain lion moved on. They stop by regularly to inquire about an apple or two now that the trees have no fruit or leaves. I still don't know if there is a particular call to action that our relationship summons from me. But as ongoing unraveling continues to trigger my anxiety, I look out my window and Mary is staring at me and then she buckles her front legs, then her back, and lies down. And Marta too. Their restful presence is a prayer inviting me into the sacred presence. I suddenly remember a conversation with a particular oak tree many years ago. She said to me, "Stop and love what is right before you." May we all awaken to her invitation to recognize the sacred presence in our glorious world.

Acknowledgments

My deep gratitude to my amazing children, Olivia Grace and Alec James: you guys are the ones who taught me to listen to the whispers of the sacred through other beings of Earth. This book was shaped by your fierce loving support. Olivia, your brilliant editing and workshopping skills made this story a coherent one—I've learned so much from you. Alec, your commitment of hours and hours to help sentences make sense and stop me from exaggerating was a blessed act of reciprocity. You both helped me grab the Muse and hold her tiny feet to the page until clarity came. Thank you for your affirmation and love throughout the whole process.

To my sister, Valerie Serrels, my best friend and basket buddy and fellow Church of the Wilder, who has been imagining this book with me for several years. I am so grateful you are always on my side, always my companion. No matter what.

I'm indebted to my mama, Joy Luna, who came to the rainy place to support me and make me many dinners while I sat at the table and wrote day after day. I love you, Mama. You made the long days easier and more enjoyable.

And to Russell Greene, my BFF and chief supporter, you always know when to text me with the exact right poem. Thank you.

My colleagues at Seminary of the Wild, Bryan Smith, Brian Stafford, and Matt Syrdal: thank you for your patience and support throughout this intense process. Your passion in this wild spirituality work gives me courage and energy every day. And to all the Seminary of the Wild participants and friends, particularly those in my Cottonwood and Vast Sky clans in the first two cohorts of the Eco-Ministry program, it has been my privilege to wander along the path with you on the edges of the edge. You are creating the field of spiritual ecology with your lives and work.

I am in awe of you remarkable Wild Church Network pastors who are all trailblazers and prophets and wisdom holders: you are the ones putting Thomas Berry's vision into practice. Thank you especially to Valerie Serrels, Wendy Janzen, James Ravenscroft, LeAnn Blackert, and Carmen Ramirez, who stepped in to help keep the network going while I was immersed in writing. Thank you, Steve Kennedy, for your openhearted support and for reading the whole draft with great feedback.

Thank you and I miss you, brave ones who helped launch the first Church of the Wild in Ojai: John and Laurie, Gina and her girls, Ken, Joanne, Lisa, Tim and Char. And a bow of gratitude to Julie Tumamait-Stenslie: the *enote-wot* (Chumash for "woman chief") rattle you made and presented to me is the most cherished piece on my altar. I'm still intimidated using it, but your confidence in me gives me courage. Thank you. And appreciation to Charis and Dianne and Emma and the whole Echoes congregation who invited me to launch Echoes Wild Church in Bellingham.

I am grateful for the guidance of Bill Plotkin and Geneen Marie Haugen who taught me many of these nature-based practices which expanded my spirituality and changed my life.

Mary Reynolds Thompson, thank you for helping me take seriously my commitment to "write the damn book!" You helped me recognize my own voice. Mirabai Starr, you helped me believe that my feminine story was important. This book made it into book form thanks to my amazing editor, Valerie Weaver-Zercher, who saw the vision, believed in me and this message, and made it happen. I am so grateful for Louisville Institute, who believed in the wild church movement enough to award me a Pastoral Study Grant in 2017 to begin writing this book.

And so much gratitude to Mary and Other Mary and Marta and Maggie and the other deer who began as muses and friends and have become family.

Resources

The Wild Church Network

Over the years I began to meet people who, like me, were leaving buildings to connect directly with the wild as a practice of church. We started meeting together via videoconference with no agenda other than to encourage one another, share ideas, and celebrate and commiserate with one another as we created new practices. As more people joined the calls from around the continent, we heard again and again, "I thought I was the only one doing this." We began to realize that we were part of something much bigger than our small experimental gatherings. Innovation often happens like this. The vision of wild church was given to many of us independently, at around the same time. So after several months, we claimed an identity: we became the seeds of the Wild Church Network. The network has since helped wild churches to blossom into a collaborative movement.

About that time, *Harper's Magazine* published an article about this emerging wild church movement. Writer Fred Bahnson described us this way: "As Western Christianity undergoes its identity crisis—a reformation or a slow implosion, depending on your leaning—a small but determined number of people . . . are urging the church to seek God in the literal wilderness."

Since 2016, we've seen the number of wild churches multiply, and more and more people are connecting with the network, looking for guidance to start their own wild churches. We tell them that what we offer is less how-to trainings and more invitation to storytelling. Each church is unique to the leader, the human community, and the bioregion where they gather.

Margaret Wheatley, speaking of the phenomenon of organic social change, asserts that "[Pioneer efforts] developed by courageous communities become the accepted standard." My wild church friends across the network have been defining the field. While the movement is still on the edges, I have no doubt that the efforts of the pioneering wild church leaders will be deeply influential. They're the wisdom keepers for the movement.

The Wild Church Network tries hard to be a container for what is emerging naturally, resisting the temptation to drift into the traps of a dogmatic institution that decides who is in and who is out and what to do and how. What is emerging through us is still becoming. It's too early to try and define it. I've just been paying attention these past few years to the many diverse expressions of what we are calling wild church. And noticing what is common.

While diverse in expression, style, and particulars of theology, we share a united sense of calling, purpose, and roots in three areas: Wild church is practiced outside. The leaders (and some of the participants) are generally those who are edge walkers on either the inside or the outside edges of the Christ tradition. And we are committed to inner and outer transformation.

Wild churches meet outside. That part is essential. Some meet in parks or off trails on the edges of their town. It's not always untamed space. Sometimes it's right in the middle of a Costco parking lot to watch the crows roost, like we did when I visited the Salal and Cedar wild church community in Vancouver, British Columbia. Some wild churches have their own land right in the middle of a suburb. Some are privileged to meet in the woods or in an oak grove. Even urban spaces are still connected to the stars, the rain, the wrens, and the dandelions that insist on existing even when their natural habitat has been concreted over.

Some churches with their own land can create large outdoor labyrinths for contemplative walking, open to the neighborhood. Some host community garden space. Others have created a Stations of the Cosmos, which guides people through sixteen billion years of evolution starting with the big bang, with each emergence in time marked at a proportionate distance along the path. What is common for those with land—and this can be done at any church with their own land—is a practice of asking the land and the beings who live there what they desire. Wandering through the space with an open heart, asking of the sacred presence there, the trees and stones and squirrels: "What is needed here? How can we be of service to this land?

What can we do to facilitate conversation between all the members of this beloved community?"

Wild churches meet in all kinds of weather. Most will only cancel services if the hills are burning or the roads are iced, which is becoming more and more of a reality with extreme heat and cold, hurricanes, wildfires, blizzards, flooding, and other climate impacts. But all kinds of weather in all seasons is part of the reason we gather outside. Our disconnection from weather and gnats and sunrises is a tragic loss that we seek to reclaim. Even the uncomfortable parts are important aspects of aliveness to experience in this place, at this moment in time. It is an act of resistance against a culture that has severed human participation in the whole system of life and prioritized comfort over connection.

We're edge walkers from the Christ tradition. We say "from the Christ tradition" because most of the leaders have come from there. But it doesn't mean that all wild churches are explicitly Christian; indeed, many, if not most, of the participants would not identify that way. The focus on our collective belonging to the world is more the core identity than any religious affiliation. That said, some wild churches are pretty mainstream Christian, like New Life Lutheran Church in Dripping Springs, Texas. While the majority of the wild churches are led by ordained ministers within one of several denominations, New Life is one of the only wild churches officially registered within a religious institution. Their community is also the only one that began as an indoor church and made the intentional transition to wild church. They moved onto a twelve-acre plot of land in the middle of a busy suburb. With more than seventy humans gathering weekly, they bring in chairs, a sound system, and shade for the hot Texas summers. The congregation follows the common lectionary, which is a prescribed set of weekly Scripture references and liturgies that Lutherans and other mainline churches follow. But their liturgies, sermons, songs, and sacraments are offered from a nature-based lens.

Three Rivers Forest Church in Ontario, Canada, and Shenandoah Valley Church of the Wild in Harrisonburg, Virginia, are decidedly Celtic. Celtic Christianity has remained distinctive in staying connected with its pre-Christian roots of reverence for the earth. James Ravenscraft and Valerie Luna Serrels, the leaders of these two churches, orient their year around the Celtic calendar, celebrating the seasonal solstices and the equinoxes, as well as the cross-quarter festivals, which are the celebrations between the seasonal shifts. Beltaine, for example, is a fire festival, welcoming the beginning of summer, falling on May Day eve.

Other wild churches are more explicitly interspiritual and include readings from many different traditions along a theme. One of them is called Integral Church in Florida. Led by Joran Slane Oppelt, organizer for the Creation Spirituality Communities that align with the teachings of Matthew Fox, Integral Church meets in local parks with music and readings from several religious traditions. Eddie Sloane, now a campus minister at Villanova University, started Wild Church West Virginia as part of their Catholic Committee group. The liturgy was a straight-up

Roman Catholic mass, adapted to include the congregants from the wild space where they were meeting. But nearly half of their human congregants were Hare Krishnas, who resonated with the reverent respect Eddie's church offered to the natural world. I can't think of any better place to meet for Advent than the New Vrindaban cow sanctuary, where they met in 2017.

We seek inner and outer transformation. Wild spirituality is a commitment to restoring inner and outer reconnection to the web of life where we already belong. Attending to the beings and places that are suffering from a lack of love is often integrated into wild-church life. Through practices that reacquaint people with their ecological grounding, wild church invites people into direct and interconnected relationship with the waters, trees, wildlife, hills of their own homes. They are oriented to a spirituality of place, where the natural world invites us into intimacy with the sacred. And the sacred invites us more deeply into relationship with the wild. Mountains and prayer are practiced together.

But the contemplative practices of the gatherings only have meaning and weight if they actually change your heart and your way of interacting with the world. The inner transformation of contemplative spirituality is connected directly with the outer transformation of our physical homes. Wild churches often encourage active engagement with and resistance to a culture that continues to devastate Earth. These actions, too, are called "church" and are part of wild spirituality.

Some churches build community gardens in empty lots or on their own land, inviting neighbors to connect with their food more directly. Some are deeply engaged with activism, showing up as a religious community to protest against coal trains and clear-cutting that desacralizes our remaining forests. Some communities focus on restoring land that has been abused.

Salal and Cedar in British Columbia focuses on activism at the center of their identity, while Bamboo Encounter in Chattanooga, Tennessee, is explicitly contemplative. Both are needed. Contemplation and action are not dualistic options. Both inner and outer transformation are essential in any relationship of love.

The wild churches blooming all over the continent are helping to create the field of spiritual ecology as they grow. You can learn more about them and find an updated list and a map of wild churches in North America at https.// WildChurchNetwork.com.

A Communal Practice of Church of the Wild

The Conversation: Ojai Church of the Wild was the name of the first wild church I started along with a small group of brave souls. It was an experiment, an opportunity to develop spiritual practices of conversation with the natural world within community. We started meeting under an oak tree near the river's dry wash, on land that had been cherished and cared for by Chumash people for more than ten thousand years. It was Advent 2015, and the group of about twenty-five of us ventured into *terra incognita*, unknown territory, with a sense of adventure. Eager to repair our own relationship to our home landscape, we also discovered a sense of deep belonging to the whole world as wildly sacred.

For our first year, a group of between twelve and thirty of us met weekly. Every other week, we met at a particular oak tree so that we could get to know this place in all seasons. We learned when the creek stopped flowing late in the summer and which flowers bloomed first in spring. In the interim weeks, we would gather along other trails, parks, and public places on the outer edges of our town. Once a month, we would meet in the evening for Taizé chanting and silent meditation as the sun set.

Every gathering, curious new people would join us. The constellation of spiritualities was always varied: people who identified as traditional Christian to agnostic to anti-Christian atheist to Buddhist to Jewish to new age to whatever. Gathered together on the land, though, religious affiliations were meaningless. We were a community through our connection with Spirit and Earth.

My friend Julie Tumamait-Stenslie is a Chumash elder whose family has lived in the Ojai region of California for more generations than she can count. She says that squirrels used to be able to jump from oak tree to oak tree for fifty miles, from the foothills of the Topatopa Mountains all the way to the ocean. I can't even imagine that now. The remaining oak trees are truly magnificent—stunning, majestic, wise beings. They are preening creatures, proud. They need to be treated with full elder respect. Even the younger ones. But they live together in only a few small groves, scattered miles apart. Even the trickiest squirrels would only be able to travel, at most, two hundred yards at a time.

I wish I could bring you there and we could experience wild church together. Perhaps the best way to share with you what we normally do during a wild church service is to invite you into a typical service. Let's try it.

* * *

On this Sunday, a group of people carrying folding chairs and water bottles are heading toward one of the most beautiful remaining oak elders for our Church of the Wild service. Usually we meet at a younger oak on the other side of the dry river wash. But it is early spring, and the river is flowing, so it's impossible for the older participants to cross. So instead we are following a path next to scattered oak trees and knee-high grasses and wildflowers on land owned by the Krishnamurti Foundation. We are heading to a particular tree who is a very close friend. I call her Mama Oak.

She is a very large live oak tree that looks like a scruffy bush from a distance. But when you get close, you notice there is a small, inviting entrance through the branches, facing west. A little vine, a rogue weed with chutzpah, is growing right over the entry as if to welcome you. Tucking your head to enter, you have to gasp just a little when you stand straight again and take in Mama Oak's enchanted interior space.

Looking up, you see a maze of ancient branches, nests, and oak leaves creating a space that feels instantly sacred, like the sense you get when you enter a medieval cathedral whose architecture mirrors the awe felt in a towering old growth forest. Or like the Mahabodhi Temple, built to literally house a tree.

Trees have been revered as sacred by humans for most of history. Inside the crown of Mama Oak, you feel deliciously invisible. If you are quiet enough, people walking their dogs beside the tree don't even notice you. Her arms, branches as thick as most tree trunks, are thick and heavy and reach all the way down to the ground. Her branches offer built-in pews, alive ones, shared with lizards, bugs, and scrub jays, easy for five or six people to sit together. Awe settles into slower breathing, and you can almost feel your heart rate recalibrating with the tree's holy rhythm.

Under Mama Oak's shade, we complete a circle and begin to build a little altar with a cloth I made, along with leaves, stones, and sticks we collect nearby. I set out a glass jar of homemade grape juice and apples someone brought from their backyard tree. The six children and teens scramble into the arms of the ancient tree through her ladder of branches. They listen with intermittent giggles from above as we begin the service with a welcome and explanation of what we are (and are not) doing out here.

Evan, the littlest human present, is just old enough to walk from person to person across the circle. Twenty years earlier I led a home church, and my own little ones were just barely school age. I had the sense that sending children out for their own children's church was not right, and I tried a bunch of different, cool things to create an engaging experience for the kids. It never worked. With wild church, however, teens and tiny ones participate fully, without a need for separate activities or cool-enough music. The children climb rocks and trees, collect leaves, find bugs, and make fairy houses and forts within hearing distance. And they listen more carefully than I imagined. The toddlers are the only ones who pose a challenge. They require a parent to walk around with them because sitting in a circle makes zero sense to someone who is newly able to walk on their own and already in love with every grasshopper and stick.

We choose to sit facing one another in a circle for the first part of this service. Sometimes, for other services, we'll face out toward each direction—north, west, south, east. I see my primary role as the one "holding the space," a term that is almost too trendy, but I can think of no better phrase. Holding space is the kind of leadership

I've learned from my deer friends. Deer are a matriarchal species. The leader is an elder doe who holds the space for the herd, confident in her own assessment of the dangers but otherwise uncontrolling. I want to create a safe, yet uncomfortable, environment that invites people to step into the unknown, encounter the sacred presence for themselves, and learn to trust their experiences. The blue jays are the preachers. And the river. And the trees and squirrels and the rusty tin can half-buried in the dirt.

We have a particular order of service that we generally follow. It begins with arriving at our site, gathering in a circle, and listening in silence. Then, there is an invocation and land acknowledgment and some music and a poem or story. The sermon takes up the majority of the time, and it has three parts: the invitation, a forty-five-minute- to hour-long solo wandering on the land, and a circle to share our experiences. We close with some kind of gratitude, sometimes communion, and a wild blessing.

* * *

The Gathering and Silence. When everyone feels settled, I transition us into more ceremonial space by inviting a time of listening. It's not really silence, though, because the land is alive with activity. It's more like inviting our own inner silence. We are here to listen to the conversation already going on in this dry chaparral terrain. As in any conversation, silence is necessary to listen to the voices of the others with all of our senses: to feel the prickly thistles digging into our legs; to observe the gnats circling this interesting warm-blooded new life in their space; to watch the wind waltzing with the leaves; to smell the oak-infused sage growing near us; to hear the distant laughter of kids playing in the houses nearby. And to open our imagination to listen in on the underground mycelium that whispers between the trees. I say words that go something like this:

> Listen to your breath. Listen to the wind. We are connected through the breath of God. Slowly allow yourself to relax into this welcoming place. You belong here with this oak tree and the stones and the flies and scrub jays and poison oak. Listen for the water, arteries of life flowing throughout the planet mirroring the arteries of blood flowing through your own body. You are a welcome part of this ecosystem. They welcome us because they have not forgotten that we are related, that we come from the same dust and return to the same dust. Take another deep breath of gratitude to acknowledge that our lives are fully dependent on the healthy functioning of this particular bio-system.

I invite us to take deep, grateful breaths, with an awareness that the presence of God is often described as the *ruach*—the wind, the breath—and how our own breath is literally dependent on the breath of the tree.

Usually there are visitors each time we gather, curious people who need to see for themselves what this wild church is all about. I spend a little time at the beginning of each service with an orientation, letting them know that this isn't just a regular church that relocated outside. I say things like,

> We aren't just meeting *in* nature; we are entering *into* relationship with nature. And in doing so, we realize that "nature" is a bit of a misnomer, actually. It implies that we aren't part of nature, that we exist outside of it and we have to learn how to get back in. A better way to see it is to recognize that we humans are already very much part of nature, we are creatures *of* (not simply in) the natural world. We are here to re-member ourselves back where we belong. We are here as an expression of religion, which means *re* (again) and *ligio* (connection). Like ligaments that hold the bones of the world together, religion simply means reconnection. We are here to restore a loving and kindred relationship with the rest of the natural world, as spiritual practice.

* * *

The Land Acknowledgment. Almost every wild church begins with a land acknowledgment to honor the watershed, the land and creatures, and the peoples who traditionally lived on this land for generations. My sister, Valerie, leader of Shenandoah Valley Church of the Wild in Virginia, wrote a land acknowledgment invocation, and I adapted it for my watershed, newly devastated by wildfire. I share it here as an example of wild church liturgy.

We offer thanks to the congregants living in the ecosystem that is unique to the Ventura River Watershed, in Ojai, the Chumash word for *moon*:

To the soil, small pebbles, and flat stones who offer the ground we stand on, to the ashen remnants of the forest that is gone, and to the giant slabs of rock that create these mountains. *We honor the sacred in you.*

To the Ventura River flowing beneath and, still in places, above the ground, delivering waters through the canyons and floors, from the mountain range through the valley and into the ocean. *We honor the sacred in you.*

To this nurturing survivor, Mama Oak, under whose protective arms we rest, and the many trees of this community, the cottonwood and oak, manzanita who have perished in the Thomas fire and those who are resolutely surviving. To the new shrubs, grasses, flowers, seeds, and plants gaining new steadiness even in this drought and the mycelium cords connecting and caring for the whole meadow. *We honor the sacred in you.*

To the rabbits, raccoons, squirrels, and deer; the scrub jays and wrens and fishes; insects and frogs; and to all individuals who lost their lives in the fires and those who survived and continue to build homes and thrive through this watershed. *We honor the sacred in you.*

To the ancient Chumash peoples, who have tended and lived in harmony with this land for over ten thousand years, to acknowledge, with grief, their suffering at the hands of missionaries and colonizers who enslaved, objectified, and nearly completely destroyed them. And to our own indigenous ancestors, some from faraway lands, who live in and through us still. *We honor the sacred in you.*

And in learning to honor the holiness in the others who are not human, may we learn to honor the sacred within ourselves and in all peoples. May we honor one another and honor life itself and sacred Mystery, Christ within all things, holding us all together, amen.

Notice that we are not inviting the trees to join us in worship, as many liturgies for creation do. We are opening up our own awareness that the trees and jays and clouds are *already* in a state of worship—simply by being themselves. They are inviting *us* to join the worship they live every day. The mountains, bushes, soil, insects, and ancestors are all acknowledged, honored, and included as cocongregants in the invocation prayer. And naming and acknowledging our watershed with gratitude helps us remember that we are utterly dependent on the gift of living water. Our cities are named by political boundaries rather than the waterways.

We honor, in particular, the ancestral human caretakers of this land. This is a practice common to nearly all wild churches. The tree where we are sitting now was once a gathering place for the Indigenous Chumash peoples, who have lived in kindred relationship with this land for nearly ten thousand years. Chumash elder Julie Tumamait-Stenslie tells us that this tree is where her grandmother once played, near her home along the river. She, along with her father and great-grandmother and great-great-grandmother for many more than seven generations, lived in an active, sacred relationship on this land.

The Franciscan mission in nearby Ventura nearly wiped out her people in an effort to control them and use them as laborers. The Chumash culture and their way of life never recovered. It is important for us to specifically and intentionally remember and honor their ancestral presence and reckon with their tragic story.

* * *

Sacred Readings. At least half of the humans gathered are decidedly not Christian, and I have no agenda to change that. Since I walk on the edges of the Christian tradition, I don't try to pretend I am anything else. When I share Scriptures, I say things like, "From my tradition, there is an ancient story about a Father who loved his two sons. One of them felt the need to see the world and asked for his inheritance before his father was even dead." I include poetry from Rumi and Mary Oliver and invite stories from others who bring wisdom from their cultures and traditions.

A poem or story or an ancient prayer is a way to ground our experience and prepare us to enter into sacred conversation. Today I bring this quote from Bonaventure, a medieval Franciscan: "Christ has something in common with all creatures. With the stone he shares existence, with the plants he shares life, with the animals he shares sensation, and with the angels he shares intelligence. Thus all things are transformed in Christ since in the fullness of his nature he embraces some part of every creature."

But the primary "readings" come from what Bonaventure called the primary book of revelation, "The Book of Creation." Not like the allegory at the end of the New Testament kind of Revelation, but revelation as insight and disclosure of the nature of God. From the Middle Ages through the Enlightenment, nature was revered as a sacred text. Saint Bonaventure, a Franciscan teacher, found revelation of the nature of God through all beings, as his spiritual teacher, Saint Francis, taught.

Each week, those who have musical talents are invited to lead or perform songs. I love it when this happens because they can often come up with songs to deepen the theme that emerges from within the circle. Simple songs that don't need printouts or hymnals are best. Some wild churches have drum circles.

* * *

Sermo: The Sermon as Conversation. The sermon is a series of conversations, honoring and restoring the original meaning of the Latin word, *sermo*, used to translate *logos*. I'm not sure exactly when *sermo* came to mean the one-sided non-conversation we call a *sermon*, but I am determined to restore conversation as a central spiritual practice.

The conversation/sermo has three parts. First, I offer an invitation to wander. Second, there is a solo wandering for a long while, off-trail, where the clouds and the water and the bugs and the live oaks are our preachers. The third part is coming back together to share what you experienced with the others in the circle. Time together and time in solitude are both valued. Time listening to the land and time listening to one another are both valued. We are practicing an ancient art of holy listening.

I thought I was making up this format, adapting practices I had learned from nature-based soul work I'd done with Animas Valley Institute, mixed with contemplative Christian practices I'd learned through the years. But a surprising number of wild churches, without consulting one another, created a similar order of worship that includes a period of time for contemplative wandering and sharing. Even those churches that are more liturgical and formal often include a time of contemplative wandering: a spiritual practice that reconnects people to the beloved community that extends beyond our own species.

Sermon part one: invitation. I spend a little time offering a few practices to help participants engage in conversation with the other beings of this place. The invitation may relate more specifically to the reading or the theme, but this time I'm just offering a basic invitation to engage with the land.

Listening to your body is the place to begin. In order to wander, you need to listen to where you are feeling drawn. And that listening doesn't happen through your ears or through your head at all. It is a heart listening. Open your imagination and invite your intuition to guide you. When you leave this circle, you may have an idea about where you want to go. *To the river! To the hilltop!* And on the way to following through on your plans, you may notice a tug stopping you or turning you the other direction. Life is like that. Listen to the tugging.

Look for what might be alluring you to cross as a threshold. A broken branch to step over? A small creek? A rusting and broken barbed-wire fence? When the threshold beckons, don't question yourself. Just follow. Surrender your plans. Forget about the instructions I'm giving you right now, even! There are no "shoulds." Follow your heart's guidance.

Before you cross the threshold, though, take a few deep breaths. Look at where you are, turn around and look at where you've been. Make an inner decision to open up your imagination, to treat this threshold as an invitation into what Celtic spirituality calls "a thin place," where the distance between heaven and Earth grows thin and the sacred can be sensed more viscerally. When you cross over, may you be open to a holy presence, beckoning you to draw closer. It may be the water's edge you had in mind when you started. It may be a barbed-wire fence caught from the corner of your eye. It could be a single green leaf on a dying branch or the ant you passed, carrying a load much too large for her.

Open up your imagination and intuition to sense who or where may be beckoning you. Ask permission to be there, to sit down and join them.

When you are there, use your senses to wonder. Praise this other, notice what is unique and alive and special about them. Tell them. Either out loud or quietly in your mind or journal it or embody it in a dance. Let them know. You may be the only human who has noticed and paid appreciative attention to this particular lizard. Like when you pay full attention to a child or your dog, and you see their eyes come alive. Let us assume all beings feels the same. Even if your brain can't wrap itself around it.

And then, release the words and sit in silence to listen. Allow any thoughts to float through you, like clouds. I like to imagine the distracting thoughts disappear like clouds shifting. With deep inner kindness, release the distractions. Smile a little when you realize it's happening. "Ha, there I go again." And with a breath, release again.

You may sense a question arising. Ask it. And see what comes up for you. Enter into the conversation. Open up to the possibility that the Conversation, which created all things and holds together all things, is present between you and this other being. Journal or simply be present in the exchange. And from this receptive posture, ask where you might be most needed today, this week. Is there anything that may be asked of you? Ask, and pay attention throughout the whole week. Let the encounter work in you.

And, when it is time to return, offer a gesture of gratitude. Indigenous peoples often left gifts of tobacco for the water or the land. Your gift could simply be a poem or smile or a respectful bow. Your tears may be the gift. Your full attention is also a gift. Ask if there might be something you can take back to the circle to share at the altar. If it feels right, bring a stick or a flower or the rusty tin can back with you, cross over the threshold again, and return here in forty-five minutes.

I know that what the congregants experience will often be completely unrelated to my particular invitation. I may invite them to "wander into a place that feels safe and speak to the land about your fears," for example—and then nobody comes back with anything remotely related to this invitation. That's fine. Each person has a unique experience and receives precisely what they need. But I've tried not giving an invitation at all, and it felt empty. So I just trust my process of preparing an invitation, and I trust their process of listening and responding.

Sermon part two: wandering and wondering. The first time I invited people to wander, I didn't explain it much. They were like, "Talk to a rock for twenty minutes? You call this church?"

"Just try it," I said confidently, as if I knew what I was doing. "The only requirement is that you not second-guess yourself. Follow where you feel drawn, sit down, and listen."

What surprised me was that when they came back, every one of them said, "We need a lot more time!" Even people who have been practicing centering prayer or meditation for years are surprised how calming and spiritually meaningful the quiet, intentional conversations can be with the natural world.

I stay behind as the people head out to wander. I hold the space at the circle. There is enough of an invitation right here, under Mama Oak, for me. The gnats are circling around my head, and as I whack the air with irritation, I realize that my entire relationship with them is annoyance. I've never once regarded them as beings with their own intrinsic value and worthy lives. So I write a poem about them, honoring their presence, and I listen to them. "What is so important that you must scream in my ear, small gnat?"

Seeing these little gnats as beings with their own lives and agendas changed my relationship with them. And while I don't like them buzzing in my ear, I am not so reactive about it anymore. And I think of all the little things in my life to which I react with annoyance rather than listening.

For forty-five minutes, congregants wander off-trail, allowing their curiosity and inner compass to lead them into an encounter. Some may sketch at the creek. Others write poems. Some are moved to tears but don't really know why. Some lie down and watch the clouds or fall asleep.

There are many ways to affectionately engage with the natural world as a sacred practice. After naming a couple dozen incredible and strange creatures, Annie Dillard declares in one of my son's and my favorite passages from *Pilgrim at Tinker Creek*, "Look, in short, at practically anything—the coot's feet, the mantis's face, a banana, the human ear—and see that not only did the creator create everything, but that he is apt to create *anything*. He'll stop at nothing."

Sermon part three: witnessing. I don't have a drum or a loud chime to call people back, though many wild churches do. So I developed an effective and entirely holy church bell. I've quite perfected my peacock call. I first did it to be funny, but I am pretty good at it! And it's loud and recognizable, and it became a thing: a ritual in itself. The Peacock Bell Tower.

After forty-five minutes, the peacock call signals people back, and they wander slowly back to the circle, bearing gifts from the land. These gifts—flowers, rocks, leaves, branches, bones from a creature who died during the recent fires—are added to the altar with a sense of reverence. It's an ephemeral altar, sometimes a mandala: gifts offered from the land and from the people to God. I say something like,

> Place your gift on the altar, and you are each invited to share a little about your experience as we pass this rock around the circle. When you receive the rock, it is your turn to share. This part of the sermo/conversation is important. Sometimes you can't see the meaning or value of an encounter until you speak it and the rest of us witness your voice. Sometimes what the others share deepens your own experience. I don't know why it works this way, but it does. A few ground rules:
>
> *Speak from your heart.* Allow your words to arise spontaneously when it is your turn to speak. And when you share, share the essence of the experience with as few words as possible. Read from your journal if you desire. Pass if you want to.
>
> *Listen from your heart.* Imagine a small circle of silence around you as you listen to the others. This is your gift to them, being as fully present to them as you can. Don't be distracted thinking about what you're going

to say. When they are finished, a word of affirmation, like "Amen," is appropriate. But resist the temptation to give advice or try to help them figure anything out. Just listen with your full attention.

The youth are often the first ones to share. My daughter, Olivia, had stopped going to church a few years earlier, uncomfortable with what she felt was inauthentic in the church. But at Church of the Wild, she is all in. After wandering, she returns with these lines: "Branches lean on one another and cry. A bird lives here. Still. Then quick. I try to crawl and venture more into this small world. I do not think I belong here. Where in God do we not belong?"

Often people share the way the wind felt or how they were drawn someplace totally unexpected. Heading toward the water, one man is distracted by the barbed wire tightening around a growing tree. Honoring that pull, he settles down before the barbed-wire tree. Then he notices the way the tree is actually taking over the wire rather than the other way around. He realizes, as he shares it with the group, that he can shift perspective about a constricting relationship in his life.

* * *

Communion. A scrub jay has been making her way closer and closer to our gathering until she lands in the middle of the circle, eyeing us. Cocking her head, she looks at us one at a time. How can we continue our own human conversation and ignore her? She clearly has come to share her story. This jay knows us. She is particularly invested in this gathering. I believe she thinks she is an usher, friendly and welcoming in her greeting of each human congregant, ready for the communion bread she knows is coming.

The sacrament of communion opened up for me once I opened up to the idea of honoring the "communion of subjects" that Thomas Berry talks about. The sacrifice of Jesus is the sacrifice of all life: for any being to remain alive, another one must die. Someone notices that the prickly dead oak leaves, poking us, is Mama Oak's offering of composted nutrients for the tree. A ritual of shared bread and wine symbolizes our common commitment to life, including the reality and necessity of death. The sacrifice of others and the sacrifice of ourselves is an expression of divine love that Jesus demonstrated. And we are invited to live with intention and wonder at the miracle of the interconnected whole. A whole that includes us all.

> What we are doing here is the embodiment of true communion. We acknowledge that we are, together, one body in Christ: each of us, this oak tree, the mountain, every stone and wren. The ancients called this interconnecting reality, Christ. Other cultures call it kindred reciprocity, the *Logos*, the *Tao*.
>
> When Jesus broke bread and shared it with his friends, he said, "This is my body given for you," as a reminder of his sacrifice. But that is not the whole message. He invites us to do the same: to sacrifice our lives for others. This is the way life works. For each being to stay alive, another being must die.

This bread required the lives of wheat; seeds of sunflowers that could have become new sunflowers instead are given to us. This wine is from the death of the grapes. Each apple's life given for each deer. Each deer for each mountain lion. Our lives, too, are asked to be given to provide life for others. Someday our physical lives will become life for others. And before then, this ritual asks us to say yes, I receive this bread and this wine, a symbol of the love of Christ poured out for me, and I offer my flesh and my blood, in love, for others. We are all connected. This is the mystery embedded in all of life.

With this bread and this wine, we remember the new covenant that God is incarnated not just in Jesus but in all of us. We are all the embodied reality of Christ, the divine in human form.

By sharing this bread and wine, we are saying yes to the true reality that one must die for another to live. We are saying yes to a reciprocal commitment to one another, to the others not in this circle, to the earth. To God.

Participation in this communion ritual is a dynamic reminder that we are already one with God. We are already the body and blood and hands and words of Christ in our world. Jesus, the person, was the embodiment of the Christ two thousand years ago. And now we, too, are the embodiment of the Christ in our world.

Jesus took the bread, gave thanks, and shared it, urging them to deliberately recall this sacred moment. And so we do also. Take from the loaf and the cup with these words: "You share the body and face and love of Christ with all beings. Take this to remember."

* * *

Benediction: Wild Blessings. Benedictions are blessings offered at the end of a religious service. The traditional one goes like this: "The Lord bless you / and keep you; / the Lord make his face shine on you . . . / and give you peace," which is nice. Another version includes the charge "Go into the world in the name of Christ," which is nice too. But after a while, they just become words to me, and my mind glazes over. The cadence, more than anything, is comforting.

A benediction in wild churches is a call to go back to the human world and to bring the lessons of the wild world with you. One song written by my friend and cofounder of Ojai Church of the Wild, John Slade, has become the defining hymn of Church of the Wild. I use it as a benediction sometimes. I sometimes bring a small speaker and play the song through my phone. The song and the man who wrote it capture the essence of wild church for me. John's song as wild blessing reminds us who we are, where we belong, and what we are doing here.

God on the outside, endlessly spacious
Ageless, audacious, fecund and wild, I am
Laid low and humbled, awed by the Splendor
Let me remember: I am the Universe's child

God on the inside, and in all places
Forever gracious, love without end

Witness inside me, see all that I see
Silently guide me
Your love includes me and transcends

God is the love that never ends.

* * *

When I moved away from Ojai, the Church of the Wild there continued as Julie Tumamait-Stenslie took over spiritual leadership. I am grateful she was willing to do so. Settler populations have so much to learn from the Native peoples of this continent about what it means to live in sacred relationship with Earth and one another. We need to learn from them, partner with them if possible, and engage in conversation. I think relationship is the only way to address potential appropriation. If you accidentally step over a line, apologize and change and grow.

I live now in Bellingham, Washington, where our church of the wild sanctuary is a circle of second- or third-generation big-leaf maples and Douglas firs in a small but magical forest next to Lake Whatcom. Or our cathedral is a city park, next to the playground, covered with snow. Sometimes we meet on the shore of the bay, among drift-wood logs we used for benches as the cedar tea brews and we gather blackberries growing on the pathway for com-munion. These are places so alive and diverse that even Cascadians, people who live in the Pacific Northwest and are accustomed to being surrounded by stunning beauty, awaken to the gift of living in a place whose wildness can still be remembered.

Listening in contemplative awe, we share our stories with one another, creating spiritual practices that connect us back into the web of life where we have always belonged. And we call this church.

Terra Divina

This practice is derived from an ancient monastic practice of *Lectio Divina*, a contemplative "divine reading" of holy Scripture. Following the same stages of immersion, *Terra Divina* is a "divine conversation" with the sacred land. You can use it on your own, to connect to the wild places near you, or in a gathering that you lead.

To prepare, pack a bag with water, sunscreen, a hat, and an emergency whistle if you'll be somewhere particularly remote. If you will be wandering in the wilderness on your own, make sure someone knows where you're going and when to expect you back. Bring your journal and maybe a backpacking chair if you have one, or a small blanket or coat to sit on.

Go to a wildish place that seems to be calling you. Someplace new? Someplace that has been beckoning you? You will know. Trust the idea that comes hopping into your mind.

When you get there, begin to wander. At some point, allow yourself to sense when it is time to cross a threshold, which could be stepping off the trail or walking under a branch on a tree or stepping over a stone. A threshold is an intentional way to tell yourself (and all the others) that you are breaking out of your regular way of seeing and stepping into a more present, more receptive mindset and a slower, more attentive way of moving.

Before you cross the threshold, hold your hands to your heart or your palms together in a deep bow of reverence. Maybe you will close your eyes. Pray in the way that feels native to you. Pray in a way that alters your everyday vision and expectations. Make a vow that you will surrender, if even for this short time, your regular ways of rushing words through your brain and rushing your body through the path. Pray a blessing over the others; let them know you come in peace.

If you can, take off your shoes. This can help you walk gently and slowly and will remind you that you are not disconnected after all, though you may have feared sometimes that you are. Your tender feet meeting hot sand or prickly rocks remind you that you are a creature of this sacred place, vulnerable and small, even as you remember how important your full presence and participation is in the whole story.

In *Lectio Divina*, the Scripture passage is read three times, and then a time of silence is offered between each stage, deepening engagement with the passage. *Lectio Divina* is not about finding the correct theology or reading but is an invitation to enter into the sacred aliveness in the text. For *Terra Divina*, each of the stages offer a parallel invitation to enter into the sacred aliveness of the "first book of God," which the ancients called nature.

1. **Wander (*lectio*).** Wander, as if wandering with your whole body and all your senses were like reading a book with your eyes and mind alone. You are reading the language of the breeze and birds and leaves and sunlight. Wander with full presence and sensuality. This step creates the space for someplace or someone or even a color or a sound to

capture your attention. Make note in your journal about where your attention is lingering.

Touch. Be aware of the way your body moves, how each step moves you closer and also farther away, how the wind touches your cheek and your hair just as she (the wind) caresses the leaves on the trees. May every step be intentional and soft, connecting with the ground solidly before lifting the other foot.

Look. Soften your eyes to look on all the beauty, the composting death alongside the new growth. Slowly, and with a posture of appreciation and praise, scan the close-up and the faraway.

Listen. When the chatter of your inner conversation blocks your ability to listen to the outside voices, tenderly sweep aside the words with a deep breath. Listen closely to the voices and songs near you, in the trees, in the plants, in the water perhaps. The voices of the birds. The movement of the other hidden ones. The gnats singing in your ears. Listen to the sounds close and far away—the human ones too. Just listen. That's all.

Breathe. Breath intentionally. Take deep breaths. Draw your attention to the way you normally breathe without thinking. Is your breath usually shallow or deep? What smells ask for your attention? Does the air have a taste?

2. **Listen (*meditatio*).** *Meditatio*, in the ancient monastic *Lectio Divina* way, is the phase of the prayer where you wonder why you might have

been drawn to the word or phrase in the text. In *Terra Divina*, this is the time for deep listening to the land and to the others whom you may have been drawn to sit and meditate with. Rather than wondering silently with your own thoughts, enter into conversation with this other. Risk it. Where have you been drawn? A mountain cliff? The bank of a small creek? The clouds gathering speed above you? A group of ants focused on transporting a leaf across the path? Move closer and settle down on the ground before or near them. *Ask permission* to sit and converse with this particular other.

Observe. Using all of your senses, offer your full attentiveness to this other. Look carefully and closely. What is moving? Who is in relationship with whom? Listen closely. Then listen farther away. Get up close and smell. Maybe even taste, if it looks safe. Lie down on your stomach and look very closely, and then flip over and look as far as you can into the sky. Feel, really *feel*, the earth, with all of your senses.

Imagine. Invite your imagination to guide you. When you watch the tree or the cloud movement or the little wren bringing a bug back to her nest, what might be happening? How is this tree connected to the earth? What does it look like beneath the soil? How many creatures met here, and who has been born here or died here? Do any unexpected words or images come to mind? Is a story starting to be told?

Mirror. Sacred reciprocity is practiced every day. When we feel loved by someone, our hearts soften, and we automatically feel love back. When someone is speaking quietly, whispering, we automatically start whispering to mirror them. Do this. Mirror the other's movements and sounds. Get up and move or dance or chant in a way that mirrors them. How might they be mirroring you?

Praise. Notice deeply and praise in your own words or heart. Maybe you can write a poem or sing or draw or simply list all of what you appreciate and see in this other. Be specific—we all like to receive praise in this way.

3. **Respond (*oratio*).** This is the stage at which you allow the resonance to conjure up a response within you. Engage fully in the new relationship, with an open heart.

Voice. As you respond to the other or others, share what is coming up for you. If possible, speak your voice in your own language, or translate it into an embodied movement or song. Or create a dialogue in your journal.

Memories. What memories are coming up? They might seem random, but pay attention. Journal about them or talk about them out loud.

Feelings. What is your body feeling? Is there a longing to do a cartwheel? Laugh? Or curl up in a ball and sob? How can you express these feelings? What emotions are coming up? Where are they located in your body? Acknowledge these. Be curious and allow all emotions that arise.

4. **Release (*contemplation*).** Now . . . let it all go. Release with a huge breath, put down the journal, shake off the emotions. Step into the sunshine. Lie down against the tree. Feel the pure gratitude of being alive, of being held, of connection. Take deep breaths, and speak something like Julian of Norwich's words to yourself: "All shall be well, and all shall be well, and all manner of things shall be well." Allow this receptive, contemplative connection to fill you as you sit or lie on the land for at least five minutes.

Gratitude. Before you go, offer gratitude. A gift of your pure presence for this sacred conversation. Leave a gift of a bit of your hair or read to them from your journal or simply offer a deep bow of appreciation.

Threshold crossing. Cross over again as you reenter the world of your adult responsibilities. Recognize how you are a bit more of yourself than you were before, thanks to this opportunity to encounter the sacred through this experience. Amen.

Notes

Chapter 1

3 **"such gifts"**: Mary Oliver, "The Place I Want to Get Back To," in *Thirst: Poems* (Boston: Beacon, 2007), 35.

7 **"We are in trouble"**: Thomas Berry, quoted in Mary Evelyn Tucker and Brian Thomas Swimme, "The Next Transition: The Evolution of Humanity's Role in the Universe," in *Spiritual Ecology: The Cry of the Earth*, ed. Llewellyn Vaughan-Lee (Point Reyes, CA: Golden Sufi Center, 2013), 59.

8 **"lethal combination"**: Carol Wayne White, "Black Lives, Sacred Humanity, and the Racialization of Nature, or Why America Needs Religious Naturalism Today," *American Journal of Theology & Philosophy* 38, no. 2–3 (May–September 2017): 111, https://doi.org/10.5406/amerjtheophil.38.2-3.0109.

9 **"collection of objects"**: Thomas Berry, *Evening Thoughts: Reflecting on Earth as Sacred Community*, ed. Mary Evelyn Tucker (San Francisco: Sierra Club, 2006; Berkeley, CA: Counterpoint, 2010), 17. Citations refer to the Counterpoint edition.

9   **"I used to think":** Gus Speth, quoted in Monty Don, "Religion and Nature," October 1, 2013, in *Shared Planet*, BBC Radio 4, MP3 audio, 0:41, https://tinyurl.com/2nwahwse.

11   **"but ask the animals":** Author translation.

11   **"Let the heavens":** Ps 96:11–12.

12   **"Morning is glad":** Opal Whiteley, *Opal: The Journal of an Understanding Heart*, adapted by Jane Boulton (New York: Macmillan, 1976; Palo Alto: Tioga, 1984), 92, 83. Citations refer to the Tioga edition.

14   **"O most honored":** Hildegard von Bingen, *Causae et Curae*, trans. Priscilla Throop, 2nd ed. (Charlotte, VT: MedievalMS, 2008).

14   **"I've adopted this term":** Benjamin Webb, *Fugitive Faith: Conversations on Spiritual, Environmental, and Community Renewal* (New York: Orbis, 1998), 163.

15   **"the narrow space":** *Encyclopedia of Religion and Nature*, ed. Bron Taylor (London: Continuum, 2005), s.v. "Williams, Terry Tempest (1955–)," 1752.

15   **"a network or group":** Wiktionary, s.v. "karass," last modified September 21, 2020, 03:40, https://en.wiktionary.org/wiki/karass.

17   **"A mystic is someone":** Samantha Vincenty, "Signs You Might Be a Mystic," *O, The Oprah Magazine*, June 17, 2019, https://tinyurl.com/4oodlxp9.

17   **"A recent study":** *"Nones" on the Rise: One-in-Five Adults Have No Religious Affiliation*, the Pew Forum on Religion & Public Life (Washington, DC: Pew Research Center, 2012), 57, https://tinyurl.com/2lozpkhg.

18   **"Christian axiom"**: Lynn White Jr., "The Historical Roots of Our Ecologic Crisis," *Science* 55, no. 3767 (March 1967): 1206, https://doi.org/10.1126/science.155.3767.1203.

22   **"Wild church re-places"**: Ada María Isasi-Díaz, "Kindom of God: A Mujerista Proposal," in *In Our Own Voices: Latino/a Renditions of Theology*, ed. Benjamín Valentín (Maryknoll, NY: Orbis, 2010), 177.

Chapter 2

29   **"That sweet night"**: *Saint John of the Cross, Dark Night of the Soul*, trans. Mirabai Starr (2002; repr., New York: Riverhead, 2003), 24.

34   **"And the land was chaos"**: Gen 1:2, author translation. The Hebrew word translated as "hovering" in most translations of this passage is the verb *rachaph*, which means "grow soft, relax, move Gently, also cherish, and brood," according to the *Brown-Driver-Briggs Hebrew and English Lexicon* (Peabody, MA: Hendrickson, 1996), 7363.

41   **"Alec's voice was already"**: Lee van der Voo, *As the World Burns: The New Generation of Activists and the Landmark Legal Fight against Climate Change* (Portland, OR: Timber, 2020), 141.

47   **"You know that the antidote"**: David Whyte, *Crossing the Unknown Sea: Work as a Pilgrimage of Identity* (2001; repr., New York: Riverhead, 2002), 132.

47   **"According to a recent study"**: Maria Nita, *Praying and Campaigning with Environmental Christians: Green*

Religion and the Climate Movement (New York: Palgrave Macmillan, 2016), 140.

48 **"A *USA Today* article"**: Sara Weissman, "God Competes against Mother Nature on Sundays," *USA Today*, August 9, 2015, https://tinyurl.com/dhqu74l3.

48 **"personal, subjective"**: Todd W. Ferguson and Jeffrey A. Tamburello, "The Natural Environment as a Spiritual Resource: A Theory of Regional Variation in Religious Adherence," *Sociology of Religion* 76, no. 3 (Autumn 2015): 297, 299, https://doi.org/10.1093/socrel/srv029.

Chapter 3

57 **"A voice of one calling"**: Isa 40:3.

57 **"A voice of one calling"**: Matt 3:3.

57 **"prepare the way"**: Mark 1:2–3, author translation.

60 **"The early church"**: Lisa E. Dahill, "Into Local Waters: Rewilding the Study of Christian Spirituality," *Spiritus: A Journal of Christian Spirituality* 16, no. 2 (Fall 2016), https://doi.org/10.1353/scs.2016.0023. This publication was Dahill's presidential address to the Society for the Study of Christian Spirituality, delivered at the November 2015 gathering of the American Academy of Religion in Atlanta, Georgia. This address appears also, slightly revised, as "Rewilding Christian Spirituality: Outdoor Sacraments and the Life of the World," in *Eco-Reformation: Grace and Hope for a Planet in Peril*, ed. Lisa E. Dahill and James B. Martin-Schramm (Eugene, OR: Cascade, 2016), 177–96.

60   **"the storied Jordan":** Ched Myers, "Water Is Life: Re-
      placing the Sacrament of Baptism," AllCreation.org,
      https://tinyurl.com/y9e66r4q.

61   **"Therefore I led them":** Ezek 20:10.

62   **"so that the accusing one":** Matt 4:1, author translation.
      The Greek word used here (διάβολος) is usually trans-
      lated as "the devil" but the actual meaning is "slanderous,
      accusing falsely." As a noun it means "the accusing one,"
      which opens up the meaning to me. James Strong, *Strong's
      Exhaustive Concordance of the Bible*, 15th ed. (New York:
      Abingdon-Cokesbury, 1944), 1228.

62   **"You know the one":** Brené Brown, "Listening to Shame,"
      TEDTalk (Long Beach, CA, Long Beach Performing Arts
      Center: TED2012 Full Spectrum, March 2, 2012), video
      shared by TED Ideas Worth Spreading, https://tinyurl
      .com/2nk2gscz.

63   **"Depth psychologist":** Bill Plotkin, *Wild Mind: A Field
      Guide to the Human Psyche* (Novato, CA: New World
      Library, 2013), 127–52.

63   **"He was with":** Mark 1:13, author translation.

65   **"Every other reference":** This isn't *every* telling of Jesus
      praying, but here are a few: Matt 14:23 (Jesus dismissed
      the crowds and went *into* the mountain alone to pray);
      Matt 26:36, Mark 14:32, and Luke 22:39 (all use *eis*
      to describe how Jesus brought the disciples with him
      into the garden in Gethsemene or the Mount of Olives);
      Mark 1:35 (Jesus departed *into* a solitary place to
      pray); Mark 6:46 (Jesus took leave of the crowds he'd just
      fed with loaves and fishes, sent the disciples to the other
      side of the lake, and departed *into* the mountain to pray);

Luke 6:12 (Jesus went out *into* the mountain to pray and spent the night praying); Luke 9:28 (Jesus brought Peter, John, and James up *into* the mountain where he was transfigured); Luke 23:46 (Jesus committed himself *into* the hands of his Father at his death). The few times the preposition *in* is used to describe where Jesus went to pray are instances when the location is the focus: Luke 5:16 (Jesus withdrew to [the location of] the wilderness to escape the crowds who wanted him to heal them of their sicknesses); Luke 9:18 (Jesus was in the middle of praying, with no specified location, when he asked the disciples who people said that he was); and Luke 11:1 (Jesus was praying *in* a "certain place" when the disciples asked him to teach them how to pray).

66   **"God said to Jacob":** Gen 28:15–16 WEB.

Chapter 4

70   **"Therefore I am now going":** Hos 2:14.

71   **"born to occupy":** Bill Plotkin, *Nature and the Human Soul: Cultivating Wholeness and Community in a Fragmented World* (Novato, CA: New World Library, 2008), 31.

71   **"there you can be sure":** David Whyte, "Sweet Darkness," in *House of Belonging* (Langley, WA: Many Rivers, 1997), 23.

73   **"The part of ourselves":** "*Courting the Wild Twin* by Martin Shaw," Chelsea Green, https://tinyurl.com/3nvfwpbo.

73   **"irresistible because she possesses":** Plotkin, *Wild Mind*, 106.

74   **"My dove in the clefts"**: Song 2:14; 6:3.

75   **"Away back"**: Albert W. Palmer, "A Parable of Sauntering," Sierra Club, https://tinyurl.com/288jdltd.

77   **"Reverence bestows dignity"**: John O'Donohue, *Beauty: The Invisible Embrace* (New York: Harper Perennial, 2005), 31.

78   **"What you encounter"**: O'Donohue, 23–24.

85   **"Yahweh is in this place"**: Gen 28:16 WEB.

Chapter 5

89   **"The heavens declare"**: Ps 19:1–3, author translation.

89   **"We are talking"**: Thomas Berry with Thomas Clarke, *Befriending the Earth: A Theology of Reconciliation between Humans and the Earth* (Mystic, CT: Twenty-Third, 1991), 20.

90   **"I began to realize"**: "David Whyte: The Conversational Nature of Reality," April 7, 2016, in *On Being with Krista Tippett*, podcast, MP3 audio, 7:24, https://tinyurl.com/condo8od.

91   **"We're surrounded"**: Belden Lane, *The Great Conversation: Nature and the Care of the Soul* (New York: Oxford University Press, 2019), 4.

91   **"For my part"**: Belden Lane, "Trees Communicate with One Another. I'm Trying to Listen," *Christian Century*, July 25, 2019, https://tinyurl.com/tm6yechh.

92   **"By instrumentalizing nature"**: Robert Macfarlane, *Landmarks* (New York: Penguin, 2016), 25.

92   **"grammar of animacy"**: Robin Wall Kimmerer, *Braiding Sweetgrass: Indigenous Wisdom, Scientific Knowledge, and the Teaching of Plants* (Minneapolis: Milkweed Editions, 2013), 5.

92   **"recognized not only"**: Robin Wall Kimmerer, "Nature Needs a New Pronoun: To Stop the Age of Extinction, Let's Start by Ditching 'It,'" *YES!*, March 30, 2015, https://tinyurl.com/7e5vx52u.

92   **"nothing place"**: Macfarlane, *Landmarks*, 15.

97   **"a continuous intersubjectivity"**: Ursula K. Le Guin, *The Wave in the Mind: Talks and Essays on the Writer, the Reader, and the Imagination* (Boston: Shambhala, 2004), 188.

98   **"She observes"**: Craig Foster and Swati Thiyagarajan, dir., *The Animal Communicator*, featuring Anna Breytenbach (Cape Town: Natural History Unit Africa, 2012).

99   **"Listening is not a reaction"**: Le Guin, *Wave in the Mind*, 188.

102   **"Grief and love are sisters"**: Francis Weller, *The Wild Edge of Sorrow: Rituals of Renewal and the Sacred Work of Grief* (Berkeley, CA: North Atlantic Books, 2015), xvi.

102   **"I could talk aloud"**: Howard Thurman, *With Head and Heart* (San Diego: Harvest, 1979), 9.

102   **"When I was young"**: Thurman, 7.

103   **"There were times"**: Howard Thurman, *A Strange Freedom: The Best of Howard Thurman on Religious Experience and Public Life*, ed. Walter Earl Fluker and Catherine Tumber (Boston: Beacon, 1998), 90.

103   **"we will recover"**: Thomas Berry, *The Great Work: Our Way into the Future* (New York: Bell Tower, 1999), 49.

104   **"if you love"**: "George Washington Carver," George Washington Carver Museum & Cultural Center, https://www.carveraz.org/gwc/.

Chapter 6

105   **"In the beginning was the Logos"**: John 1:1–3, 14, author translation. *Logos* is the Greek word nearly always translated as "word." It will become clear through this chapter why I chose not to translate it for this opening epitaph. The Greek word, οὗτος, is translated in just about every single other use in the New Testament as "this" or "these things." While most translations of John 1:2 decided for theological reasons to translate οὗτος as "He," I choose to rely on the actual meaning of the word, and so I use "this."

106   **"tied in a single garment"**: Martin Luther King Jr. to Bishop C. C. J. Carpenter et al., Birmingham City Jail, April 16, 1963, 2, The Martin Luther King, Jr. Research and Education Institute, Stanford University, https://tinyurl.com/43hwwu8n.

106   **"In the beginning God created"**: Gen 1:1.

106   **"a divine reason"**: *Encyclopaedia Britannica Online*, s.v. "Logos," updated May 20, 2020, https://www.britannica.com/topic/logos.

107   **"As an intellectual"**: Christopher Lyle Johnstone, *Listening to the Logos: Speech and the Coming of Wisdom in Ancient Greece* (Columbia: University of South Carolina Press, 2009), 216–17.

107 **"organizing, integrating":** Antonía Tripolitis, *Religions of the Hellenistic-Roman Age* (Grand Rapids, MI: William B. Eerdmans, 2002), 37.

108 **"underlying the structures":** Kay Keng Khoo, "The Tao and the Logos: Lao Tzu and the Gospel of John," *International Review of Mission* 87, no. 344 (January 1998), https://doi.org/10.1111/j.1758-6631.1998.tb00068.x.

109 **"Up until the fourth century":** Majorie O'Rourke Boyle, "Sermo: Reopening the Conversation on Translating JN 1,1," *Vigiliae Christianae* 31, no. 3 (September 1977): 161, https://doi.org/10.2307/1583129.

109 **"which means not 'word'":** *Oxford Classical Dictionary Online*, s.v. "sermo," by John Wight Duff and M. Winterbottom, https://doi.org/10.1093/acrefore/9780199381135.013.5850.

109 **"the divine indwelling":** John 1:3.

109 **"extends a tradition":** Boyle, "Sermo."

110 **"Jesus, for John":** Richard Rohr, introduction to *Oneing: The Universal Christ*, ed. Vanessa Guerin (Albuquerque, NM: CAC, 2019), 2, 4.

110 **"Christ is not Jesus' last name":** Richard Rohr, "Creation as the Body of God," *Radical Grace* 23, no. 2 (April–June 2010): 3.

111 **"In the beginning":** John 1:1–3, 14, author translation, based on Erasmus's 1519 translation and Greek text.

112 **"A subatomic particle":** Fritjof Capra, "The New Vision of Reality: Parallels between Modern Physics and Eastern Mysticism," *India International Centre Quarterly* 9, no. 1 (March 1982): 17, https://tinyurl.com/yknzhsmy.

113 **"The forest is not a collection"**: David George Haskell, *The Songs of Trees: Stories from Nature's Great Connectors* (New York: Viking, 2017), 17.

113 **"English is a nounbased language"**: Kimmerer, *Braiding Sweetgrass*, 53.

115 **"Where two or three"**: Matt 18:20, author translation. The Greek word μέσος means "in the middle, in-between, in the midst." Usually, translations use "there I am in the midst of them," but "there I am in between them" is also an accurate translation.

116 **"single supreme authority"**: Lexico.com, s.v. "empire," Oxford University Press, https://www.lexico.com/en/definition/empire.

117 **"The Romans relentlessly mined"**: Wes Howard-Brook, *Empire Baptized: How the Church Embraced What Jesus Rejected* (Maryknoll, NY: Orbis, 2016), 32.

117 **"a religion of creation"**: Throughout his book *Empire Baptized*, Howard-Brook pits the "religion of creation," initiated by Jesus, against the "religion of empire," which Christianity became.

118 **"Take off your shoes"**: Ex 5, author translation.

118 **"I am who I am"**: Ex 3:14.

122 **"*Sermo* . . . more perfectly"**: Erasmus, in Boyle, "Sermo," 167.

123 **"The model of the world"**: Sallie McFague, "Imaging a Theology of Nature: The World as God's Body," in *Liberating Life: Contemporary Approaches in Ecological Theology*, ed. Charles Birch, William Eaken, and Jay B. McDaniel (Maryknoll, NY: Orbis, 1990), 226.

125 **"a change in language":** Benjamin Lee Whorf, *Language, Thought, and Reality: Selected Writings*, ed. John B. Carroll (1956; repr., New York: John Wiley & Sons, 1959), 263.

Chapter 7

128 **"People exploit":** Wendell Berry, *Life Is a Miracle: An Essay against Superstition* (2000; repr., Berkeley, CA: Counterpoint, 2001), 41.

131 **"Do not arouse":** Song 3:5.

131 **"Only in risking":** Lane, *Great Conversation*, 4.

139 **"Knowing that you love":** Kimmerer, *Braiding Sweetgrass*, 124–25.

140 **"I knew it with a certainty":** Kimmerer, 122.

141 **"In the end":** Baba Dioum, in JoAnn M. Valenti and Gaugau Tavana, "Report: Continuing Science Education for Environmental Journalists and Science Writers," *Science Communication* 27, no. 2 (December 2015): 308, https://doi.org/10.1177/1075547005282474.

141 **"We cannot protect":** Richard Louv, *The Nature Principle: Human Restoration and the End of Nature-Deficit Disorder* (Chapel Hill, NC: Algonquin Books of Chapel Hill, 2011), 104.

141 **"You can't lead":** Cornel West (@CornelWest), Twitter, December 5, 2013, 11:46 p.m., https://tinyurl.com/vc4bw2vh.

Chapter 8

154 **"originating or occurring"**: Lexico.com, s.v. "indigenous," Oxford University Press, https://www.lexico.com/
en/definition/indigenous.

154 **"In an open letter"**: Robin Wall Kimmerer, "The
Windigo," in *Dear America: Letters of Hope, Habitat,
Defiance, and Democracy*, ed. Simmons Butin, Elizabeth
Dodd, and Derek Sheffield (San Antonio, TX: Trinity
University Press, 2020), 55.

155 **"Greater love has no one"**: John 15:13.

155 **"My friend, ecotheologian Lisa Dahill"**: Lisa E. Dahill,
"Eating and Being Eaten: Interspecies Vulnerability as
Eucharist," *Religions* 11, no. 4 (April 2020): 205, 212,
https://doi.org/10.3390/rel11040204.

157 **"The divine indifference"**: Belden Lane, "Fierce Landscapes and the Indifference of God," Religion Online,
https://tinyurl.com/52248von.

158 **"Whoever wants to save"**: Matt 16:25.

158 **"All goes onward"**: Walt Whitman, *Song of Myself* (New
York: BN, 2008), 6.

159 **"Just as cells"**: Andreas Weber, *Matter and Desire: An
Erotic Ecology* (White River Junction, VT: Chelsea Green,
2017), 67.

162 **"what opens up"**: Michael Dowd, Post Doom (website),
https://postdoom.com.

163 **"acquainted me"**: Gerald May, *The Wisdom of Wilderness: Experiencing the Healing Power of Nature* (New York:
HarperSanFrancisco, 2006), xx.

164 **"Describing a night"**: May, 31, 32.

164 **"It is not enough"**: Kimmerer, *Braiding Sweetgrass*, 327.

167 **"would bring a different kind"**: Stephanie Kroner, "Etty Hillesum, 'Life Is Beautiful, in Spite of Everything,'" Unitarian Universalist Church of Berkeley, 2015, https://tinyurl.com/gu38vq7f.

168 **"I have looked"**: Etty Hillesum, *An Interrupted Life: The Diaries, 1941–1943 and Letters from Westerbork* (New York: Owl, 1996), 155, 294.

Chapter 9

170 **"with a change of worldview"**: Mary Evelyn Tucker, "Biography of Thomas Berry," *Minding Nature* 2, no. 3 (Winter 2009): 22, https://tinyurl.com/3ruhu5pp.

170 **"the largest story"**: Plotkin, *Wild Mind*, 2.

170 **"something I can't not do"**: Parker J. Palmer, *Let Your Life Speak: Listening for the Voice of Vocation* (San Francisco: Jossey-Bass, 2000), 25.

171 **"engage in conversations"**: "Coming Home to an Animate World: A Way of Ceremony and Conversation—August 2019," Animas Valley Institute, https://tinyurl.com/u5pawdb2.

174 **"a force that will actually take you"**: Elizabeth Gilbert (@GilbertLiz), "DEAR ONES—Question of the day: Are you allowed to exist?," Facebook photo description, November 30, 2014, https://tinyurl.com/azpnbs2r.

175   **"to assist the world"**: Michael Meade, *The Genius Myth* (Seattle: Green Fire, 2016), 12.

179   **"Earth is currently suffering"**: Weber, *Matter and Desire*, 3.

180   **"I was no longer"**: John Seed and Joanna Macy, *Thinking like a Mountain: Towards a Council of All Beings* (Gabriola, BC: New Society, 1988), 1.

182   **"Nature was unsafe"**: Veronica Kyle, "Eco-Womanism for the Church," Wild Luminaries webinar, Seminary of the Wild, December 3, 2020, https://tinyurl.com/140y0w2o.

184   **"the voices of women"**: Melanie L. Harris, "Introduction: Ecowomanism: Earth Honoring Faiths," *Worldviews* 20, no. 1 (January 2016): 1, https://doi.org/10.1163/15685357-02001001.

184   **"And will you"**: Episcopal Church, *The Book of Common Prayer and Administration of the Sacraments and Other Rites and Ceremonies of the Church* (New York: Seabury, 1979), 538.

185   **"Peter, do you love me?"**: John 21:17, author translation.

186   **"Joanna Macy tells this story"**: "Three Dimensions of the Great Turning," 2021, Work That Reconnects, https://tinyurl.com/59ryrvmu.

186   **"The moral of this story"**: Mark Pullam, "Native Story of Three Sisters Offers a View into These Troubled Times," Yachats News, April 12, 2020, https://tinyurl.com/3tmpvajh.

187   **"Emergence violates"**: Margaret Wheatley and Deborah Frieze, "Lifecycle of Emergence: Using Emergence to

Take Social Innovation to Scale," *Kosmos*, Spring/Summer 2015, https://tinyurl.com/4e3n628k.

The Wild Church Network

193   **"As Western Christianity":** Fred Bahnson, "The Priest in the Trees: Feral Faith in the Face of Climate Change," *Harper's Magazine*, December 2016, https://tinyurl.com/88kol1m3.

194   **"[Pioneer efforts] developed":** Wheatley and Frieze, "Lifecycle of Emergence."

A Communal Practice of Church of the Wild

209   **"Christ has something":** Bonaventure, "Sermon for the First Sunday of Lent," *The Works of St. Bonaventure* (Paterson, NJ: St. Anthony Guild, 1960), in Richard Rohr, *Eager to Love: The Alternative Way of Francis of Assisi* (Cincinnati, OH: Franciscan Media, 2014), 161.

210   **"The Book of Creation":** Ilia Delio, Keith Doublass Warner, and Pamela Wood, *Care for Creation: A Franciscan Spirituality of the Earth* (Cincinnati, OH: Franciscan Media, 2020), 18. Bonaventure was one of many early and medieval theologians who referred to creation as the first book of God.

215   **"Look, in short":** Annie Dillard, *Pilgrim at Tinker Creek* (2007; repr., New York: Harper Perennial Modern Classics, 2013), 136.

218 **"This is my body"**: Luke 22:19.

220 **"The Lord bless you"**: Num 6:24–26.

220 **"God on the outside"**: "God Outside and Inside," Lyrics page on John Slade website, track 8 on Night Crossing, 2014, http://slademan.com/lyrics/.

Terra Divina

228 **"All shall be well"**: Julian of Norwich, *Revelations of Divine Love*, ed. Grace Warrack (London: Methuen, 1911), 57.